# BRITISH STEAM PATRIOTS

Remembrance Day, also known as Poppy Day or Armistice Day is a memorial day observed in Commonwealth (British) countries to remember the members of their armed forces who have died on duty since World War 1. Remembrance Day is observed each year on 11th November. 'At the 11th hour of the 11th day of the 11th month', marking the formal end of World War. The red remembrance poppy has become the familiar emblem of the occasion. The poppies bloomed across the WW1 battle fields of Flanders and their brilliant red colour is an appropriate symbol representing the blood spilt in wars. Loco No 45500 PATRIOT is pictured decorated with poppies outside Rugby locomotive shed on November 11th 1955. *Bruce Chapman Collection/Colour Rail*

# BRITISH STEAM
# PATRIOTS

*Keith Langston*

WHARNCLIFFE
TRANSPORT

First published in Great Britain in 2011 by
Wharncliffe Transport
An imprint of
Pen & Sword Books Ltd
47 Church Street
Barnsley
South Yorkshire
S70 2AS

ISBN 978 1 84563 145 1

Typeset in 11pt Minion by Mac Style, Beverley, East Yorkshire
Printed and bound in China through Printworks Int. Ltd.

Pen & Sword Books Ltd incorporates the Imprints of Pen & Sword Aviation,
Pen & Sword Family History, Pen & Sword Maritime, Pen & Sword Military,
Pen & Sword Discovery, Wharncliffe Local History, Wharncliffe True Crime,
Wharncliffe Transport, Pen & Sword Select, Pen & Sword Military Classics,
Leo Cooper, The Praetorian Press, Remember When, Seaforth Publishing
and Frontline Publishing.

For a complete list of Pen & Sword titles please contact
PEN & SWORD BOOKS LIMITED
47 Church Street, Barnsley, South Yorkshire, S70 2AS, England
E-mail: enquiries@pen-and-sword.co.uk
Website: www.pen-and-sword.co.uk

# CONTENTS

The 3 cylinder LMS Patriot class was introduced towards the end of Sir Henry Fowler's reign as CME of the LMS, a position he held from 1925 until 1932 when William Stanier was appointed in his stead.

All the Patriots were painted out in LMS crimson lake livery with pale yellow and black lining when first built and carried 'LMS' lettering on the tenders. From 1946 most were painted out in LMS lined black with straw and maroon lining. Some Patriots kept this style of livery in very early BR days with the name British Railways written in full on the tender. All of the class were later painted out in British Railways standard Brunswick green with orange and black lining with the BR 'lion and wheel' logo or later BR crest on the tender.

Unfortunately all were scrapped by British Railway.

## LMS – 'Patriot' and 'Rebuilt Patriot' 4-6-0 Locomotive Details

| | | |
|---|---|---|
| Power Classification | 5XP reclassified 1951 to 6P5F | 6P reclassified in 1951 7P |
| Introduced | 1930–1934 | 1946–1949 |
| Designer | (Sir) Henry Fowler CBE | 18 Locos rebuilt by Ivatt |
| Company | London Midland & Scottish | LMS/British Railways |
| Loco weight | 80 ton 15 cwt | 82 ton 0 cwt |
| Tender weight | 42 ton 14 cwt | 54 ton 13 cwt |
| Water capacity | 3500 gallons | 4000 gallons |
| Coal Capacity | 5 ton | 9 ton |
| Driving wheel | 6 foot 9 inch diameter | 6 foot 9 inch diameter |
| Bogie wheel | 3 foot 3 inch diameter | 3 foot 3 inch diameter |
| Boiler pressure | 200 psi superheated | 250 psi superheated |
| Cylinders | 3–18″ diameter x 26″ stroke | 3–17″ diameter x 26″ stroke |
| Valve gear | Walschaert piston valves | Walschaert piston valves |
| Tractive effort | 26520lbf | 29570lbf |

## Year end Patriot locomotives in service (BR)

| | 1948 | 1950 | 1960 | 1961 | 1962 | 1963 | 1964 |
|---|---|---|---|---|---|---|---|
| 6P5F | 35 | 34 | 32 | 24 | Nil | Nil | Nil |
| 7P | 17 | 18 | 18 | 17 | 16 | 11 | 3 |
| Total | 52 | 52 | 50 | 41 | 16 | 11 | 3 |

# Chapter 1

# LMS 'PATRIOT' CLASS 4-6-0 LOCOMOTIVES

## Past, Present and Future!

Patriot 5XP No 45519 LADY GODIVA roars through Longsight station, Manchester in June 1957 with an express, note the superb ex LNWR signal gantry. *W Oliver/Colour Rail*

In March 2009 a group of dedicated enthusiasts took delivery of a set of newly cut locomotive frame plates. Perhaps not an earth shattering piece of information when viewed in isolation but add in all the other salient facts and you will appreciate what a great railway preservation milestone the cutting of those steel frames represents.

They were purchased by members of the LMS-Patriot Company Ltd, who with the help of public donations, have commenced the building of a completely new steam locomotive to be entirely representative of the long defunct 5XP/6P5F 'Patriot' class, in original build form. They plan to 'steam' that new engine well in time for the '100th Anniversary of the Armistice' in 2018, poignantly the new Patriot 4-6-0 No 45551 will be named THE UNKNOWN WARRIOR.

The new build Patriot No 45551 THE UNKNOWN WARRIOR is set to steam in time to celebrate the 100th Anniversary of the Armistice in 2018. The new locomotive will serve as a permanent memorial to all those who fought and died in the First World War and all subsequent wars. This was the original intention of the L. & N. W. R. Claughton memorial engine subsequently named 'Patriot' after which the class took its name. The LMS-Patriot Project aims to continue that tradition in memory of all those brave men and women who courageously served their country. The project has received the endorsement of The Royal British Legion, and No 45551 will carry a Legion crest above 'The Unknown Warrior' nameplate, in recognition of this. *LMS-Patriot Project*

In October 2008, the order for the frame plates was placed with Corus Steel. Measuring 39ft in length 4 foot high and 1⅛ inch thick, the two steel frame plates gave the new 'Patriot' locomotive an official identity for the first time. The frame plates were plasma cut to the correct shape and then machined and drilled. Thereafter they were delivered to the Llangollen Railway Works in spring 2009, where the assembly of locomotive No 5551 will be carried out. You could say that the group are following in a certain Mr Fowler's footsteps, albeit some 79 years later!

## Sir Henry Fowler

First then let us examine the origin of the ex LMS 'Patriot' class. Almost all British built steam locomotive classes are directly linked to the name of a designer and in the case of the Patriots that name is Sir Henry Fowler (1870–1938). The Henry Fowler name could well have been linked with fine furniture and not railway locomotives, had the Evesham born young Fowler chosen to follow in his father's footsteps and become a cabinet maker. He instead chose locomotive engineering and became an apprentice under John Aspinall (later Sir John) at the Horwich Works of the Lancashire & Yorkshire Railway.

In 1900 Fowler joined the Midland Railway eventually becoming assistant works manager at Derby in 1905 and works manager two years later. Fowler served as Chief Mechanical Engineer of the Midland Railway (MR) from 1909 to 1922, and then the London Midland & Scottish Railway (LMSR) from 1925 to 1930. He

LNWR Bowen Cooke designed, rebuilt with ('G9½ S' type boiler) 'Claughton' class 5XP 4-6-0 LMS No 6004 (BR 46004) is pictured with a freight train at Crewe in August 1946. This loco carried the name PRINCESS LOUISE between 1922 and July 1935 after which time that name was transferred to Stanier 'Princess Royal' class No 6204 (46204). The Claughton locomotive was withdrawn by British Railways (BR) in April 1949 and cut for scrap later that year. *Colour Rail*

previously served the LMSR as deputy CME under George Hughes and to his credit designed the highly successful 'Royal Scot' class.

He was bestowed with a knighthood for wartime service to the railways (1914–1918). Interestingly after completing his term as CME Fowler became adviser to the LMS research department's vice-president (1931 to 1933) and in that capacity he oversaw the purchase of various prototype diesel shunting locomotives, a great many of which were later introduced into traffic by the company.

## Birth of the 'Baby Scots'

During the late 1920s Fowler was occupied with trying to improve the performance of an earlier London North Western Railway design of 4-6-0 passenger locomotives known as the 'Claughton' class. The 4-cylinder Crewe built front line express locomotives never consistently delivered good performances in traffic. By 1928 Fowler had tried several modifications including the fitting of larger boilers designated type 'G9½ S', but despite the modifications the Claughtons remained erratic performers. In service the new boiler had proved to be an excellent steam raiser and clearly capable of powering other locomotives.

LMS No 5902 SIR FRANK REE is pictured at the north end of Camden shed in 1932. This loco became No 5501 in 1934 and also had a change of name in 1937 becoming ST. DUNSTAN'S. Note that the leading set of driving wheels (and axle) has been removed, presumably to facilitate repairs. The large ex Claughton wheels with enlarged centre bosses can clearly be seen. *Edward Talbot Collection*

In 1930 the LMS took a decision to rebuild two of the 'Claughton' class locos as 3-cylinder engines with 3 sets of Walschaerts valve gear. Fowler decided to use the cylinders from the already in service 'Royal Scot' class engines which incorporated long travel valves and the improved 1928 parallel boiler design, originally fitted to 20 of the Claughtons, in addition the driving wheels of the Claughtons were re-used but in truth little else.

The first two locomotives did however incorporate more of the original. All the Claughton driving wheels were pressed off their axles and re-used with a new crank axle being manufactured and located between what was originally the middle set of driving wheels. The original LNWR Crewe 6′3″ bogie was re-used. One other difference which acted against standardisation was the different wheel spacing of the first pair of axles 5′11½″, 7′5″ & 7′10″. The remainder adopted the Scot spacing of 5′10½″, 7′4″ & 8′0″, a practice which was carried through to the 'Jubilee' 4-6-0 class. The other difference lay in the springing in that the leading coupled wheels had coil rather than leaf springs.

The rebuilt locomotives were No 5971 CROXTETH and No 5902 SIR FRANK REE, both at that time retained their original name and number. The work was carried out at Derby Works. Unlike the 'Claughton' class the new locomotives were a great success and because of their close physical resemblance to the slightly larger and more powerful Fowler 'Royal Scot' class (but with lower axle loading) the new engines became colloquially known as 'Baby Scots'.

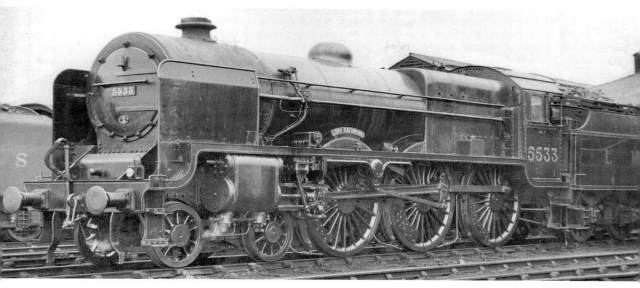

**LMS No 5533 LORD RATHMORE is pictured at Crewe North depot on 07/05/39.** *Edward Talbot Collection*

Following the early success of the first two rebuilt engines the LMS embarked in 1932 upon a building programme of 50 more 'Baby Scot' locomotives, 40 at Crewe Works and 10 at Derby Works, the two batches were constructed simultaneously. The Chief Mechanical Engineer of the LMS at that time was Sir Ernest Lemon (1931–1932) who was succeeded by Sir William Stanier (1932 to 1944).

The first 40 engines were designated as rebuilds of the life expired 'Claughton' class. However the term 'rebuild' in that instance was probably used for accounting purposes only. For although 'as built' the new locos carried the names and numbers of the Claughton 4-6-0s they replaced, few if any actual parts of the former LNWR locos were used in their construction. In direct contrast the last ten engines were officially designated as 'new build' and included no parts from withdrawn Claughton locomotives.

The new build 'Patriot' class' engines incorporated the same Stanier wheel pattern which was used on the Jubilees, as a replacement for the Scots, and as standard on the first 40 production Patriots. The Patriots were known as 'rebuilt Claughtons' and benefited from the intervention of William Stanier in a number of ways, in particular from a new design of axlebox which when retro fitted to the 'Royal Scot' class succeeded in almost eliminating instances of 'hot boxes'.

The original 'new build' order had been for fifteen locomotives but in the event the final five engines constructed (LMS numbers 5552 to 5556) were delivered by Crewe Works in 1934 with a Stanier design taper boiler, effectively becoming the first of the 4-6-0 'Jubilee' class. Known initially as 'Rebuilt Claughtons with taper boiler', they were first classified as '5XP' and then in 1951 reclassified as '6P5F'. The

BR No 45543 HOME GUARD is seen waiting to depart from Stockport with an express, the date is 19/06/59 and the loco typically looks to be in the need of a clean. *D Forsyth/Colour Rail*

Patriot No 45513 (an un-named member of the class) is pictured southbound at Crawford on the West Coast Main Line in September 1958. *David Anderson*

Carnforth based BR No 45503 THE ROYAL LEICESTERSHIRE REGIMENT commendably looks to be in pristine condition in this September 1960 image. *Colour Rail*

last Patriot No 5551 and first Jubilee No 5552 SILVER JUBILEE both emerged from Crewe Works in May 1934.

In 1935 the class was renumbered by the LMS, with numbers 5500 to 5541 being allocated to the supposed rebuilds, and numbers 5542 to 5551 allocated to the officially categorised 'new' engines. Only after the naming of loco No 5500 as PATRIOT in February 1937 (originally called CROXTETH) did the then '5XP' 4-6-0 class take on the designation of 'Patriot' class. The whole of the class were not given names and indeed various name changes took place during their working lives.

## Patriots in service

Originally the 'Patriot' class locomotives were not considered to be the exact equal of the 'Royal Scot' class and were therefore classified as '5XP', the same category as the 3-cylinder LMS 5MT 'Black Five' class. The power classification for the unrebuilt 'Patriot' class was changed to '6P5F' in 1951 by British Railways. The Patriots were to be seen at work hauling a great many of the express passenger services on both the Western and Midland Divisions of the LMS. Notably the class regularly worked the frequent London Euston–Birmingham New Street two hour expresses.

Paired with a narrow (7′1″ wide tank) Fowler 3,500 gallon tender (5½ tons of coal after the addition of coal rails) the newly introduced 'Patriot' class 4-6-0s

The driver of BR No 45516 THE BEDFORDSHIRE AND HERTFORDSHIRE REGIMENT prepares to get his train away from Manchester Exchange station in February 1959. Note the sand box, and small quantity of spilled sand on the running plate. *Keith Langston Collection*

performed well and were highly regarded engines by the crews who worked them. They soon established a reputation as fast runners and reports of speeds in the region of 93 mph were not uncommon. In fact in regular traffic the class often took on jobs normally rostered for the larger and more highly rated 'Royal Scots', and were never proved to be in any way inferior to that class.

After the formation of British Railways 'Patriot' class engines (including rebuilt versions) could be found mainly at depots associated with the West Coast Main Line with a small allocation at the BR LMR Leeds depot. One, No 45509 THE DERBYSHIRE YEOMANRY was allocated to Derby for a number of years from 1953 (the date it was named) and later numbers 45504/6 and 45519 were allocated to Bristol (Barrow Road) in 1958 surviving there until withdrawal. Later, members of the class were allocated to other locations to suit the rapidly changing traffic patterns as the end of the BR steam era approached. The first locomotive of the class to be withdrawn was No 45502 in September 1960, and the last was No 45550 in November 1962.

Double heading, approaching Colwich with a down train are MR 4-4-0 No 416 and LMS No 5505 (then un-named) in this 1934 image. This Patriot was named THE ROYAL ARMY ORDNANCE CORPS in 1947. *PS Kendrick/Edward Talbot Collection*

## Performance of the Patriots

In overall performance terms the 'Baby Scots' were on a par with the large boilered Claughtons and worked similar turns. This is really not surprising as they carried the same boiler and their power output was very similar. The big difference lay in the cost of maintenance which was substantially lower for the Patriots than for their four cylinder cousins. They had a repair cost index of 118 (as compared to a Midland/LMS Class 2 which was the benchmark100). In comparison the 4–cylinder LNWR 4 'Claughton' class scored 175 and the 'Royal Scot' 177.

Given that the 'Royal Scot' class had an almost identical chassis to the 'Baby Scots' this is surprising, although at this point in their service life the Scots did have the early axleboxes which the LMS only began to be changed after Stanier arrived on the scene. Stanier had already modified the design of the 'Baby Scots' to reflect some proven Great Western Railway locomotive building practices, accordingly and so when they entered traffic teething problems were few in number.

**Leader of the class BR No 45500 PATRIOT is pictured passing 'centre road' at Stockport on 29/10/60. Being first in the class did not earn the loco any special place in the cleaning queue although someone has chalked a spurious name on the smoke box door.** *D Forsyth/Colour Rail*

When the LMS 'Jubilee' class appeared almost immediately afterwards the difference in performance could not have been more marked, and not to the advantage of the Jubilee 4-6-0s. In the mid thirties OS Nock notes that the performance of the class was excellent particularly on the Wolverhampton–Euston and North West–Euston routes. He mentions a run from Stoke with 445 tons in tow in which following a 'stop to remove the remains of a chicken from the loco the last 97 miles to Euston was covered in 93½ minutes', a remarkable performance! Motive power depots generally reported overall satisfaction with the performance of their Fowler designed 'Patriot' class locomotives.

The 3-cylinder 4-6-0s were capable of reaching and maintaining speeds in the upper eighties and right through to the end of the 1950s were rostered on top flight

**Unnamed BR No 45547 is pictured having just passed Shotton on the North Wales main line on 18/02/61.** *Dick Blenkinsop/LMS Patriot Project*

express duty, often substituting for locomotives with higher tractive effort statistics. The class was the epitome of a well designed second string locomotive which served its two masters well in a wide variety of work over nearly thirty years (LMS 1930 to 1948 and BR 1948 to 1965).

Unlike the 'Royal Scot' class locos, there appear to have been few negative issues surrounding the integrity of the frames and apart from the rebuilds, where the first eight had new front ends and the remaining ten new frame plates, the originals remained original! Apart from loco No 45508, which received the widely lampooned BR experimental stove pipe chimney, no modifications of note were made and the un-rebuilt members of the class remained in mainly as built condition during their long and successful service lives.

LMS No 45500 PATRIOT pictured at Weaver Junction on the West Coast Main Line (WCML) with a southbound freight on 15/10/55. The flyover carries the up line from Liverpool Lime Street. *Dick Blenkinsop/LMS Patriot Project*

BR No 45517 (unnamed) is pictured taking water on Whitmore Troughs on 03/08/57. *Dick Blenkinsop/LMS Patriot Project*

BR No 45546 FLEETWOOD is pictured passing Whitmore (south of Crewe WCML) at speed on 03/08/57. *Dick Blenkinsop/LMS Patriot Project*

A very leaky kettle! BR No 45524 BLACKPOOL pictured on the WCML at Old Milverton on 07/04/53. *Dick Blenkinsop/LMS Patriot Project*

Rebuilt 6P Patriot No 45521 RHYL starts to blacken the sky on the climb to Lancaster Old with a fitted freight in June 1963. Note the Travelling Post Office (TPO) pick up point and cabin to the right. *E Oldham/Colour Rail*

## Rebuilt Patriots

In 1942 the LMS rebuilt two 'Jubilee' class 7P 4-6-0 locomotives, numbers (4)5735 and (4)5736, they were rebuilt with larger boilers, double chimneys and smoke deflectors. The design was hailed as being a great success and so led directly to the rebuilding of 18 members of the 'Patriot' class to an Ivatt inspired design between 1946 and 1949. Thus some 'Patriot' rebuilds were LMS built engines (8 locos) and others British Railways engines (10 locos), i.e. built after January 1948. All of the rebuilding work was carried out at Crewe Works.

The locos were rebuilt with the larger Stanier 2A taper boilers, double chimneys, new cylinders (based on those fitted to the Jubilees) new cabs and new tenders, later they were also fitted with curved 'Scot' type smoke deflectors. When newly built the 'Rebuilt Patriots' were given the power classification 7P. In service the rebuilds were considered to be equal in performance to the rebuilt 'Royal Scot' class locomotives but additionally were described as being 'better riding engines'. In general terms the 'Patriot' rebuilds were hardly distinguishable from the rebuilt 'Scots' and rebuilt 'Jubilee' class engines.

The eight LMS 'Patriot' rebuilds were numbers 5514, 5521, 5526, 5528, 5529, 5530, 5531 and 5540 (LMS numbers). The ten BR 'Patriot' rebuilds were numbers 45512, 45522, 45523, 45525, 45527, 45532, 45534, 45535, 45536 and 45545 (BR numbers).

Crewe Works rebuilt 'Jubilee' class' 4-6-0 7P locomotive No 45736 (LMS 5736) PHEONIX, which along with No 45735 COMET (LMS 5735) re-entered service in 1942. Both were withdrawn from service by BR in September 1964. Loco No 45736 is pictured at Carlisle Kingmoor shortly before that event in the company of a 'Jinty' and 'Black Five', also presumably awaiting their turn in the scrap line. The cabside of 'Princess Coronation' class 4-6-2 No 46226 DUCHESS OF NORFOLK can be seen in the row of engines beyond, that locomotive was withdrawn in October 1964. *Keith Langston Collection*

Rebuilt Patriot BR No 45523 BANGOR pictured with an up relief train at Denbigh Hall near Bletchley on 17/06/63. *David Anderson*

**LMS Locomotive, comparison table Patriot, Royal Scot, Jubilee, Black Five**

| Locomotive type 4-6-0 | Power Class (post 1951) | Locomotive Designer | Driving wheel | Cylinders | Boiler pressure | Tractive Effort (Lbf) |
| --- | --- | --- | --- | --- | --- | --- |
| 'Patriot' | 6P5F | Fowler LMS | 6' 9" | 3 × 18" x 26" | 200psi | 26520 |
| 'Rebuilt Patriot' | 7P | Ivatt LMS/BR | 6' 9" | 3 × 17" x 26" | 250psi | 29570 |
| 'Royal Scot' | 7P | Fowler LMS | 6' 9" | 3 × 18" x 26" | 250psi | 33150 |
| 'Rebuilt Scot' | 7P | Stanier LMS/BR | 6' 9" | 3 × 18" x 26" | 250psi | 33150 |
| 'Jubilee' | 6P5F | Stanier LMS | 6' 9" | 3 × 17" x 26" | 225psi | 26610 |
| 'Rebuilt Jubilee' | 7P | Stanier LMS | 6' 9" | 3 × 17" x 26" | 250psi | 29570 |
| 'Black Five' | 5MT | Stanier LMS | 6' 0" | 2 × 18½" x 28" | 225psi | 25455 |

*Note:* Tractive effort (also known as tractive force) is basically used in railway engineering terminology when describing the pulling power of a locomotive and the figure quoted can be either actual or theoretical and usually refers to normal operating conditions.

## Patriot tender types

Originally paired with a Fowler 3,500 gallon tender carrying 5½ tons of coal (with greedy rails added). Later in their working lives the engines received other types of tender which included the Stanier 4000 gallon, 9 ton tender and the LMS straight high-sided 3500 gallon, 7 ton tender.

**BR No 45509 THE DERBYSHIRE YEOMANRY pictured in the early morning mist at Gloucester Eastgate with a Birmingham New Street-Bristol train, November 1953.** *Dick Blenkinsop/LMS Patriot Project*

BR No 45533 LORD RATHMORE pictured passing through Acton Bridge station (WCML) with an up express on 10/03/56. Note the Stanier 8F pulling out onto the down main at the same instant. *Dick Blenkinsop/LMS Patriot Project*

Unnamed BR No 45544 seen between trains at Liverpool Lime Street station on 16/07/55. *Dick Blenkinsop/LMS Patriot Project*

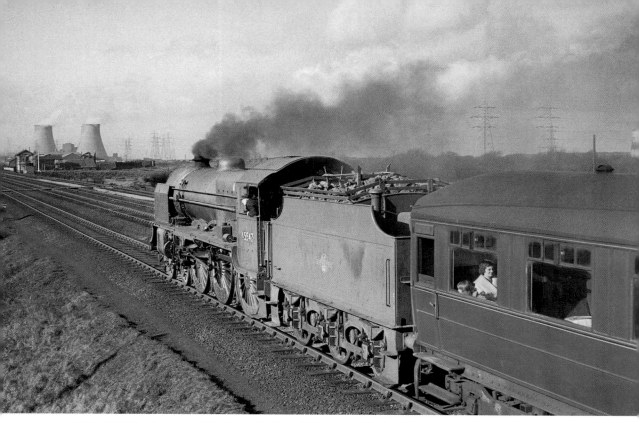

BR No 45547 has just passed Shotton on the North Wales route, 18/02/61. Something on the adjacent road seems to have grabbed not only the attention of the driver but also the youngster in the first compartment. *Dick Blenkinsop/LMS Patriot Project*

BR No 45519 LADY GODIVA with a very black exhaust, pictured at Dore and Totley in June 1960. *PJ Hughes Colour Rail*

BR No 45507 ROYAL TANK CORPS seen at Carnforth motive power depot during its last months in service. *LMS Patriot Project*

Rebuilt Patriot BR No 45545 PLANET is pictured at Crewe Station on 20/06/57. This locomotive is coupled to a Stanier 40000 gallon tender. *D Forsyth/Colour Rail*

# Chapter 2

# SUMMARY OF LMS 'PATRIOT' CLASS 3-CYLINDER 4-6-0 LOCOMOTIVES

The leader of the class 4-6-0 No 45500 PATRIOT pictured at speed on the West Coast Main Line (WCML) near Symington with a Liverpool/Manchester–Glasgow express on the 25/06/ 60. Note the driving wheels with large centre bosses, inherited from the LNWR 'Claughton' class loco it replaced. Loco No 5500 originally carried the name and number of 'Claughton' No 5971 CROXTETH, when introduced by the London Midland & Scottish Railway (LMS) in November 1930. The loco was renumbered and subsequently named PATRIOT in 1937. *David Anderson.*

## The 'Baby Scots'

In all 52 locomotives made up the famous 'Patriot' class and unfortunately not one single example was preserved. The first of the class entered London Midland & Scottish Railway (LMSR) service in November 1930 with the last of the class withdrawn from British Railways (BR) service on 1 December 1965. The locomotive 4-6-0 class (which could be said to have evolved from the London & North Western Railway 'Claughton' class) were originally all parallel boiler engines until 18 of them were rebuilt, by first the LMS and then BR, with 'Stanier' tapered boilers between March 1947 and January 1949.

When first observed in service the Crewe and Derby built 3-cylinder engines quickly earned the name 'Baby Scots' because they were strikingly similar in appearance to the Royal Scot class locomotives introduced by the LMS between 1927 and 1930. The similarity of exterior appearance continued with the rebuilt 'Scots', 'Patriots' and indeed 'Jubilee' class locomotives. The 'Baby Scots' did not become officially named as 'Patriots' until 1937 when the first built of the class received the name 'Patriot', and also took on the mantle of LNWR/LMSR national memorial engine.

When first built the Patriots were given the LMS power rating of 5XP which was changed to 6P5F by British Railways in 1951, rebuilt examples of the class were later given the BR power rating of 7P. The rebuilt Patriots were considered to be at the least equal in performance to the 'rebuilt Royal Scots' and reportedly were much better riding engines.

Those of an age may recall that lineside identification of the locomotive approaching with a fast moving train was made a little more difficult by those similarities. The cry of 'Scot', 'Pat' or 'Jub' was often followed by a hasty retraction as the passing loco had once again been momentarily misidentified! At least that was the case along the stretch of WCML between Crewe and Hartford frequented in the 1950's by the writer. Reference to my now extremely dog-eared *ABC* shows that all of the 52 Patriot numbers were underlined in that period, mostly having been 'spotted' on the aforementioned route, or alternatively observed from a favoured vantage point by the signal box at Rhyl station during holidays.

Named locomotives of that period were without doubt great aids to education, many a young enthusiasts' knowledge of Britain's far flung empire, regiments and historic past etc were perchance sharpened by their knowledge of a steam locomotive. I remember well being admonished by a teacher (whom I then considered to be akin to Attila the Hun) when in answer to the question 'where will you find Bechuanaland boy?' I replied 'in the Jubilee class sir, number 45599!' The slightest mention of that name was thereafter associated with the sharp pain caused by a direct cranial hit, sustained from a well aimed blackboard duster! What of Atilla? We became great friends in later life, especially after I discovered that he was an accomplished railway photographer. Oh happy days!

The selection of names bestowed upon 42 locomotives of the 'Patriot' class locos is to say the least interestingly diverse! If you were intent on being unkind you could even say that they represented a hotch potch of old LNWR names, which perhaps had little if any relevance to the Patriot time period, additionally the names of some extremely worthy British regiments and an assortment of references to seaside resorts etc. Hard to imagine though what kind of logic decreed that *Bunsen*

and *Lady Godiva* made the list? Furthermore who were E. Tootal Broadhurst and E.C. Trench? The names have a varying degree of historic worth and therefore a brief explanation of each is given, together with details of the locomotives.

The Patriots were originally painted in LMS crimson lake livery with pale yellow and black lining and carried 'LMS' lettering on the tenders. From 1946 onwards most of the class carried LMS lined black with straw and maroon lining. Some locomotives kept this style of livery in post 1948 BR days, often with the name British Railways written in full on the tender. Later in their lives the class received British Railways Brunswick green orange and black lined livery with the BR 'lion and wheel' logo (or alternatively the later BR crest) on the tender. Unnamed Patriot No 45547 is pictured in lined Brunswick green livery and in what looks to be ex-works condition at Willesden depot in May 1961. *S M Watkins/Colour Rail*

# Original build locomotive comparisons

**Above: Patriot 'Baby Scot' 4-6-0 No 45539 E.C.TRENCH, pictured at Stockport in May 1956. This locomotive is coupled with an LMS Straight High Sided 3500 gallon tender.** *Mike Stokes Collection.*

**Below: Compare the outward appearance of un-rebuilt Royal Scot 4-6-0 No 46134 THE CHESHIRE REGIMENT, pictured outside Dalry Road motive power depot, Edinburgh in July 1953. This locomotive was later rebuilt.** *David Anderson.*

**Note. Neither locomotive is pictured with its original LMS tender.**

# Rebuilt locomotive comparisons

**Above: February 1950 rebuilt Royal Scot Class 4-6-0 No 46107 ARGYLL AND SUTHERLAND HIGHLANDER, pictured at Glasgow Polmadie depot in February 1960. The rebuilt Patriots had their sandboxes located below the running plate whilst the rebuilt Royal Scots had theirs above the running plate.** *David Anderson*

**Below: Compare the outward appearance of January 1949 rebuilt 'Patriot' class 4-6-0 No 45522 PRESTATYN, pictured outside Buxton depot in 1964. There is however a noticeable difference in the design of the cab windows.** *Keith Langston*

The LMS-Patriot Project has teamed up with transport artist Colin Wright to produce a superb Limited Edition print of 'The Unknown Warrior' on shed at Llangollen. Limited to 500 prints, £5 from the sale of each print is being donated to The Royal British Legion in recognition that 'The Unknown Warrior' has been endorsed as the new National Memorial Engine. The print measures 27.5" x 22" (700mm x 560mm) and is hand signed by the artist and

by David Bradshaw, Chairman of The LMS-Patriot Project. A signed Limited Edition certificate of authenticity is also included. Priced at **£55 + £4.95 P&P**, all proceeds from the sale of the print will go towards completing the building of 'The Unknown Warrior'. Visit www.lms-patriot.org.uk

# Chapter 3

# THE 'PATRIOT' CLASS OF LOCOMOTIVES

A total of 52 Patriot 4-6-0 Fowler designed 5XP locomotives were built by the London Midland & Scottish Railway (LMS) between 1930 and 1934 (reclassified 6P5F in 1951). The complete class of locomotives were taken into stock by British Railways (BR) in 1948. Under BR 18 of the class were rebuilt with larger boilers, tapered chimneys and new cylinders between 1946 and 1949, they were then given a power rating of 7P.

Mileages shown hereafter include any available 'shopping' mileages, additional to annual mileage returns. The mileages have been compiled after a meticulous examination of available official Patriot engine history cards. The author is indebted to locomotive performance analyst Doug Landau who compiled the Patriot statistics and has kindly allowed his work to be published.

Patriot No 45550 is seen arriving at Manchester Exchange station in February 1959. *Mike Stokes Collection*

Original LMS number **5971**, 1934 LMS number **5500**, British Railways number **45500**, locomotive named **CROXTETH** (1930) and then **PATRIOT** in 1937. After which the class became known as the 'Patriot' class.

Principal recorded shed allocations for loco No 5500 (45500) included Camden (09/1935) Willesden (04/1944) Edge Hill (01/1948) Longsight (09/1950) Carlisle Upperby (10/1957) Newton Heath (02/1961) the locomotive was withdrawn 11 March 1961 and cut up at Crewe Works. Known mileage in service 1,210,263, (1960 details not included).

Built at LMS Derby, No 5971 entered service on 8 November 1930. This was one of two original engines from the class of 52 which were designated re-builds, having been developed from the LNWR 4 cylinder Claughton Class 4-6-0's. With hindsight the LMS use of the term 'rebuild' in relation to the first two Patriots has been proven to be somewhat misleading. The first two engines of the class did replace time expired Claughton 4-6-0s, from which they took their original LMS running numbers, but in truth little else. The most easily discernable ex Claughton feature being the driving wheels which incorporated a larger diameter centre boss

Loco No 45500 PATRIOT is pictured with an up train at Carlisle station on 3/08/57. The larger diameter wheel centres (ex Claughton) can clearly be seen in this image. The locomotive is coupled to an original design Fowler 3500 gallon/5 ½ ton coal capacity tender fitted with coal rails (greedy bars). *D Forsyth/Colour Rail*

than the newly cast wheels of the rest of the class.

A nameplate from the first of the class, which then collectively became known as 'Patriots' after the 1937 re-naming of loco No 45500. *LMS-Patriot Project*

The name *Croxteth* was of LNWR origin and it is the title of an area of Liverpool in general, and in particular, the name of a historic hall. Croxteth Hall dating from circa 1575 is the former home and country estate of the Molyneux family, the Earls of Sefton. Now owned by the Liverpool city council the hall and gardens are a popular visitor attraction, rumour has it that the building is haunted!

The name *Patriot* was originally carried by Crewe built LNWR Claughton 4-6-0 No 1914 (LMS number 5964) that locomotive entered service in May 1920 and was withdrawn by the LMS in July 1934. Some three years later the first operational so called 'Claughton rebuild' (by then seven years in service and carrying LMS number 5500) was renamed *Patriot* and thereafter became known as the LMS memorial engine. The name was bestowed by the LNWR in memory of the companies' employees who lost their lives during the First World War (1914–1918). The *Patriot* name plate additionally carried the inscription IN MEMORY OF THE FALLEN L&NWR EMPLOYEES 1914-1918, over 3 lines under the name. The venerable and then discontinued ex LNWR *Croxteth* name thereafter being confined to railway history.

Original LMS number **5902**. 1934 LMS number **5501**, British Railways number **45501**, locomotive named **SIR FRANK REE** (1930) and then **ST. DUNSTAN'S** in 1937.

Built at LMS Derby, No 5902 entered service on 13 November 1930. This was the second of the two original engines originally designated re-builds, having been developed from the LNWR 4 cylinder Claughton Class 4-6-0's. The most easily discernable ex Claughton feature being the driving wheels which incorporated a larger diameter centre boss than the newly cast wheels of the rest of the class.

The name Sir Frank Ree was an original LNWR Claughton name carried by the loco No 1191 which became LMS No 5902 and was withdrawn in November 1930, the name was in 1937 transferred to Patriot No 5530 (45530).

Principal recorded shed allocations for loco No 5501 (45501) included Camden (09/1935) Edge Hill (04/1944) Preston (01/1948) Longsight (09/1950) Longsight (10/1957) Carlisle Upperby (06/1961) the locomotive was withdrawn on 26 August 1961, and cut up at Crewe Works. Known mileage in service 1,266,774, recorded for the life of the loco.

**LMS 4-6-0 Locomotive No 5902 (original LMS number), then named SIR FRANK REE is pictured when new at Derby in this official 1930 LMS picture, The 5XP power classification is carried in a single line on the narrow section of cab, in front of the window. Note the large ex Claughton driving wheels with enlarged centre bosses.** *David Anderson Collection*

The name *St. Dunstan's* was carried on a 'badge plate' honouring the former War Blinded Association, London.

St Dunstan's to this day helps ex-Service men and women who have lost their sight, whatever the circumstances. Some St Dunstaners lost their sight during active service; others experienced an accident on a training exercise, or suffered vision problems as a result of illness or old age. Her Majesty the Queen is the Patron of the St. Dunstan's organisation and notable

The name St. Dunstan's (bestowed in 1937) was carried on a 'badge plate' honouring the former War Blinded Association, London. *David Anderson*

Vice Patrons include General Sir Peter de la Billière, KCB, KBE, DSO, MC, DL, Rear Admiral Sir Donald Gosling, KCVO, Admiral Sir Jonathon Band GCB DL, General Sir Richard Dannatt GCB CBE MC and Air Chief Marshal Sir Joe French KCB CBE FRAeS RAF.

The organisation was founded by Sir Arthur Pearson, Bt, GBE (1866-1921) who was a prominent British newspaper proprietor and publisher, perhaps best remembered for founding the Daily Express. Sir Arthur suffered failing eyesight during the early 1900s and later became totally blind. In 1914 he became president of the National Institute for the Blind and in 1915 he founded St Dunstan's Home for Soldiers, originally in order to help troops blinded by WW1 gas attacks and associated traumas.

Note. Saint Dunstan was educated by Irish monks at Glastonbury Abbey. In addition to his ecclesiastical work he was a silversmith and accomplished harpist. He was appointed Abbot of Glastonbury in 944 and Archbishop of Canterbury in 960

Patriot 4-6-0 No 45501 (BR number) St DUNSTAN'S is pictured at Bettley approaching Crewe during the summer of 1959. *Alan Fozzard*

**LMS No 5501 is pictured on shed at Willesden carrying the St. Dunstan's crest, a 1947 image the 5XP power classification is in this instance carried on the cab side panel below the window and well above the slightly smaller LMS style number. The locomotive is coupled to an original Fowler tender but at that time without 'greedy bars' (coal rails). Note also the fluted side rods which were peculiar to loco numbers 5500 and 5501.** *Edward Talbot Collection*

**LMS Patriot No 5902 SIR FRANK REE (which became 5501 in 1937) is pictured at Derby in this 1932 image.** *Edward Talbot Collection*

Original LMS number **5959**, 1934 LMS number **5502**, British Railways number **45502**, locomotive named **ROYAL NAVAL DIVISION**, in 1937.

Built at LMS Crewe No 5959 entered service on 1 July 1932 (then unnamed). The first 40 engines which were designated as rebuilds of the life expired 'Claughton' class. However the term 'rebuild' in this instance was probably used for accounting purposes only. For although 'as built' the new locos carried the names and numbers of the Claughton 4-6-0s they replaced, few if any actual parts of the former LNWR locos were used in their construction.

Principal recorded shed allocations for loco No 5502 (45502) included Camden (09/1935) Camden (04/1944) Preston (01/1948) Crewe North (09/1950) Carlisle Upperby (10/1957) Carlisle Upperby (09/1960) the locomotive was withdrawn on 3 September 1960, and cut up at Crewe Works. Known mileage in service totalled 1,388,805 (until the end of 1960).

The name *Royal Naval Division* was bestowed on the locomotive in June 1937 whilst No 5959, the Claughton locomotive it replaced (withdrawn July 1932) was

**LMS loco No 5502 is pictured approaching Colwich with a down train circa 1935, note the 'ancient and modern' mix of coaching stock. As BR No 45502 this loco was the first of the class to be withdrawn from service in September 1960.** *Edward Talbot Collection*

Loco No 5502 again pictured near to Colwich on the West Coast Main Line (WCML), the date was 24/09/1938, the ROYAL NAVAL DIVISION nameplate can clearly be seen. *Edward Talbot Collection*

unnamed. The Royal Naval Division was founded at the beginning of the First World War when it was realised that the Royal Navy had thousands of surplus sailors, even after manning all the vessels of the fleet. The military hierarchy concluded that the war would be mainly fought on land and decided not to expand the navy. Personnel from the Royal Naval Reserve, Royal Fleet Reserve, Royal Naval Volunteer Reserve, a full brigade of Royal Marines and sundry Royal Navy and army personnel were brought together and mustered at Crystal Palace in September 1914 in order to form the Royal Navy Division (RND). The new division was often referred to as 'Winston's Little Army' as it was founded by the great man when he held the position of First Lord of the Admiralty. The RND fought alongside the army, but originally flew the White Ensign and maintained naval traditions, for example being allowed to grow beards and remain seated during a toast to the King's health. When in France during 1916 the RND came under direct army control and from that time onward were known as the 63rd (Royal Naval) Division, 'Winston's Little Army' fought with great distinction. The division was demobilised in April 1919 following an inspection by the Prince of Wales and was disbanded in June of that year.

ROYAL NAVAL DIVISION nameplate in LMS livery style, also carried in BR era. *David Anderson*

Original LMS number **5985**, 1934 LMS number **5503**, British Railways number **45503**, locomotive originally named **THE LEICESTERSHIRE REGIMENT** in 1938, and renamed **THE ROYAL LEICESTERSHIRE REGIMENT** in 1948.

Built at LMS Crewe locomotive No 5985 entered service on 1 July 1932 (then unnamed). Principal shed allocations for this loco included Camden (09/1935) Willesden (04/1944) Crewe North (01/1948) Crewe North (10/1957) Carlisle Upperby (03/1961). The locomotive was withdrawn on 12 August 1961, and cut up at Crewe Works. Known mileage in service totalled 1,231,955 (until the end of 1960).

The name *The Leicestershire Regiment* was bestowed on the locomotive in 1938 and was changed to *The Royal Leicestershire Regiment* in 1948, the name plate incorporated a regimental crest. Loco No 5959, the Claughton locomotive it replaced (withdrawn July 1932) was unnamed.

The Leicestershire Regiment was raised in 1688. In 1777 it was awarded the unbroken Laurel Wreath emblem for its bravery at the Battle of Princetown, during the American War of Independence. In 1825 the Regiment was awarded the Honour of wearing the insignia of the Royal Tiger superimposed with the word Hindoostan, in recognition of its exemplary service and conduct during its campaigning and long tour in India from 1804-1823. Since that time the Regiment was always proudly called 'The Tigers'. The Regiment became The Royal Leicestershire Regiment in 1946, becoming in 1964 the 4th Leicestershire Battalion the Royal Anglian Regiment and in 1968 the 4th Battalion the Royal Anglian Regiment. The regiment which became known as Tiger Company in 1970 was subsequently disbanded in 1975.

BR Loco No 45503 carrying **THE ROYAL LEICESTERSHIRE REGIMENT** nameplate is pictured over the ash pit at Edinburgh Dalry Road Shed on 14/07/55. This view shows to good effect the similarity in appearance between the 'Baby Scots' and the 'Royal Scots'. *David Anderson*

Original LMS number **5987**, 1934 LMS number **5504**, British Railways number **45504**, locomotive was named **ROYAL SIGNALS** in 1937 and the nameplate incorporated a regimental crest.

LMS No 5504 THE ROYAL SIGNALS passing Basford Sand Sidings (south of Crewe) on 07/05/1939. *George Barlow/Transport Treasury*

Built at Crewe the locomotive entered service on 18 July 1932 (then unnamed). Loco No 5987, the Claughton locomotive it replaced (withdrawn August 1932) was unnamed. Principal shed allocations for this loco included Camden (09/1935) Willesden (04/1944) Crewe North (02/1948) Crewe North (09/1950) Carlisle Upperby (10/1957) Bristol Barrow Road (02/1962). The locomotive was withdrawn on 17 March 1962, and cut up at Crewe Works. Known mileage in service totalled 1,247,779 (up to 05/04/61).

The Corps of Signals was formed in 1920 and its history in the field of British military communications is a long and illustrious one. Swift and accurate passage of information has always been paramount to military success after all the ancient Greek armies had Torch and Water Telegraph systems whilst the Roman armies communicated with coloured smoke. A Royal Warrant was signed by the Secretary of State for War, the Rt. Hon

Royal Signals name plate complete with military crest, as carried by BR No 45505. D *Forsyth/Colour Rail*

LMS No 5987 which later became LMS No 5504 is pictured in the Crewe Works paint shop just prior to its completion in June 1932. *Edward Talbot Collection*

Winston S Churchill, who gave the Sovereign's approval for the formation of a 'Corps of Signals' on 28th June 1920. Six weeks later, His Majesty the King conferred the title 'Royal Corps of Signals'. During the 1920s and 1930s the strength of the signal 'Corps' steadily increased and during WW11 the Royal Signals had serving totals of approximately 8,518 officers and 142,472 other ranks. The 'Corps' still provide vital communications for the British military and NATO in modern times. The 'Corps' Motto is 'Certa Cito', which freely translated means 'Swift and Sure'.

BR No 45504 makes a spirited getaway from Birmingham New Street station on 02/05/1961, note the onlookers! This was one of three un-rebuilt Patriots transferred to Bristol Barrow Road in 1958 (45504, 45506 and 45519). The trio continued to work from the, by then BR Western Region, frequently working Birmingham, Derby and York services. *Colour Rail*

Original LMS number **5949**, 1934 LMS number **5505**, British Railways number **45505**, locomotive was named **THE ROYAL ARMY ORDNANCE CORPS** in 1947. Loco No 5949, the Claughton locomotive it replaced (withdrawn July 1932) was unnamed.

Built at Crewe the locomotive entered service on 26 July 1932 (then unnamed). Principal shed allocations for this loco included Camden (09/1935) Camden (04/1944) Preston (02/1948) Carlisle Upperby (09/1950) Longsight (10/1957) Lancaster Green Ayre (05/1962). The locomotive was withdrawn on 2 June 1962, and cut up at Crewe Works. Known mileage in service totalled 1,362,838 (up the end of 1961).

The name *Royal Army Ordnance Corps* was bestowed in 1947, and incorporated a regimental crest. This loco was originally allocated the name *Wemyss Bay*, which it never carried. Loco No 5949 the Claughton locomotive it replaced (withdrawn July 1932) was unnamed.

The Royal Army Ordnance Corps RAOC can trace its ancestry back to the year 1414 when a civilian 'Office of Ordnance' was created and that organisation became a Military Board of Ordnance in 1683. Under that title it supplied weapons and

**BR No 45505 THE ROYAL ARMY ORDNANCE CORPS is pictured 'on shed' at Lancaster on 17/03/1962.** *Colour Rail*

BR No 45505 is pictured 'on shed' at Stockport on 06/06/1960. Note that at this time the locomotive had lost its original Fowler tender in favour of the newer 'straight high sided 3500gallon/7 ton coal' capacity tender originally fitted to a Jubilee Class 4-6-0. *D Forsyth/Colour Rail*

ammunition to the whole British army being also responsible for the Royal Artillery (RA) and the Royal Engineers (RE) in the period up to 1855. The Field Train Department was formed in 1792 and was directly under the 'boards' control, numerous other titles were thereafter used and indeed officers and other ranks at that time belonged to different organisations. In order to clarify the situation a change in structure came about in 1896, officers were assigned to the Army Ordnance Department (AOD) whilst warrant officers, NCOs and soldiers were placed in the Army Ordnance Corps. After the end of WW1 in 1918 the two groups were merged to form the Royal Ordnance Corps which remained an independent part of the British army until reorganisation in 1993. The Corps motto is *Sua Tela Tonanti* which literally translated means 'His missiles thundering (of Jupiter)' But within the 'Corps' the historical usage was 'Unto the Thunderer his Arms' which was later changed to 'To the Warrior his Arms'

The nameplate carried by LMS 5505 (BR 45505). *David Anderson*

.

Original LMS number **5974**, 1934 LMS number **5506**, British Railways number **45506**, locomotive named **THE ROYAL PIONEER CORPS** in September 1948. Loco No 5974, the Claughton locomotive it replaced (withdrawn July 1932) was unnamed.

The name plate, which incorporated a military crest, was unveiled by Viscount Montgomery of Alamein in a special ceremony at Euston Station on 15 September 1948.

Built at Crewe, the locomotive entered service on 1 August 1932 (then unnamed). Principal shed allocations for this loco included Bushbury (09/1935) Willesden (04/1944) Carlisle Upperby (02/1948) Crewe North (09/1950) Carlisle Upperby (10/1957) Bristol Barrow Road (03/1962). The locomotive was withdrawn on 17 March 1962, and cut up at Crewe Works. Known mileage in service totalled 1,317,581, for the life of the loco.

The British Army raised the Auxiliary Military Pioneer Corps as a solo entity on 17th October 1939, for many years prior to that event several British regiments had benefited greatly from the support of their own 'Pioneer' elements. In October 1939 the Auxiliary Military Pioneer Corps (AMPC) came into being. On 22 November 1940 the name was changed from the AMPC to the Pioneer Corps. Pioneers were additionally recruited from throughout Africa, Mauritius and India. They performed a wide variety of tasks in all theatres of war. These tasks range from handling all types of stores, laying prefabricated track on the beaches, airfield building, numerous essential support duties and also stretcher bearing. In 1946, King George VI conferred upon the Pioneers the title 'Royal' for its 'meritorious work during the 1939–1945 war'. On 5 April 1993, the Royal Pioneer Corps united with the Royal Corps of Transport, the Royal Army Ordnance Corps, the Army Catering Corps, and the Postal and Courier Service of the Royal Engineers, to form the Royal Logistics Corps.

BR No 45506 THE ROYAL PIONEER CORPS is pictured at Crewe Works after an overhaul on 27/05/1956. *T B Owen/LMS-Patriot Project*

Sunshine and snow! No 45506 heads a down freight towards Penrith (WCML) in February 1957. *Ray Oakley/Colour Rail*

Original LMS number **5936**, 1934 LMS number **5507**, British Railways number **45507**, locomotive was named **ROYAL TANK CORPS** in 1937. The name plate incorporated a military crest. Loco No 5936, the Claughton locomotive it replaced (withdrawn August 1932) was unnamed.

Built at Crewe, the locomotive entered service on 12 August 1932 (then unnamed). Principal shed allocations for this loco included Bushbury (09/1935) Camden (04/1944) Crewe North (02/1948) Crewe North (09/1950) Crewe North (10/1957) Lancaster Green Ayre (10/1962). The locomotive was withdrawn on 20 October 1962, and cut up at Crewe Works. Known mileage in service totalled 1,284,746 (up to 09/05/61).

The Royal Tank Regiment was formed almost immediately after the invention of the armoured tank, British tanks were first used in great numbers during the Battle of the Somme in 1916 (WW1). At that time the six tank companies were grouped as the Heavy Branch of the Machine Gun Corps (MGC). In November 1916 eight companies (by then in existence) were each expanded to form battalions lettered

**LMS No 5507 ROYAL TANK CORPS heads an up train past Crewe Carriage Sheds on 07/05/1939.** *George Barlow/ Transport Treasury*

**BR No 45507 heads south through Stafford on 03/06/1952 with a London express.** *E R Morten/LMS-Patriot Project*

**ROYAL TANK CORPS with an up service at Hellifield in 1962.** *M Chapman/Colour Rail*

A through H; another seven battalions, I through O, were formed by January 1918, when they all were converted to numbered units. On 28 July 1917 the Heavy Branch was by Royal Warrant separated from the rest of the MGC and given official status as the Tank Corps. More battalions continued to be formed, and by December 1918, 26 had been created. On 18 October 1923, it was officially named Royal (making it the Royal Tank Corps) by Colonel-in-Chief King George V. At that time the famous motto 'Fear Naught', the distinctive black beret with unit badge were all adopted. The word Corps was replaced in 1939 with Regiment to give the unit its current name. At the time of writing the Colonel in Chief of the Royal Tank Regiment was HRH Queen Elizabeth II.

## 'Patriot' Class – The Military Connection

The great British tradition of naming steam locomotives regularly included the use of regimental names, the 'Patriot' class was no exception in addition to the National Memorial locomotive No 45500 PATRIOT ten other locomotives carried regimental names. An additional two locomotives carried the names of World War 1 Victoria Cross (V.C.) recipients.

| Loco numbers | Name and date bestowed |
| --- | --- |
| 5502 (45502) | ROYAL NAVAL DIVISION 1937 |
| 5503 (45503) | THE LEICESTERSHIRE REGIMENT 1938, renamed THE ROYAL LEICESTERSHIRE REGIMENT 1948 |
| 5504 45504) | ROYAL SIGNALS 1937 |
| 5505 (45505) | THE ROYAL ARMY ORDNANCE CORPS 1947 |
| 5506 (45506) | THE PIONEER CORPS 1948 |
| 5507 (45507) | ROYAL TANK CORPS 1937 |
| 5509 (45509) | THE DERBYSHIRE YEOMANRY 1951 |
| 5516 (45516) | THE BEDFORDSHIRE AND HERTFORDSHIRE REGIMENT 1938 |
| 5528 (45528) | R.E.M.E. 1959 |
| 5543 (45543) | HOME GUARD 1940 |

| Loco numbers | Name and date bestowed |
| --- | --- |
| 5536 (45536) | PRIVATE W. WOOD V.C. 1936 |
| 5537 (45537) | PRIVATE E. SYKES V.C. 1933 |

LMS Patriot No 5936 which entered service in August 1932 is pictured in 1935 with an up 'milk and parcels' service. This locomotive became LMS No 5507 in 1934 and was named Royal Tank Corps in 1937. It appears that the locomotive fireman has just lifted the scoop after taking water as his engine approaches the end of the 'up' water trough. The location is Hademore Troughs near to Whittington in the district of Lichfield. There was an

LNWR signal box near to the troughs at Hademore Crossing and the original top section of that box has been preserved and reunited with an appropriate brick base at the Chasewater Railway, Staffordshire. *PS Kendrick/Edward Talbot Collection*

Original LMS number **6010**, 1934 LMS number **5508**, British Railways number **45508**, the locomotive was unnamed. Loco No 6010, the Claughton locomotive it replaced (withdrawn September 1932) was also unnamed.

Built at Crewe, the locomotive entered service on 8 August 1932. Principal shed allocations for this loco included Bushbury (09/1935) Willesden (04/1944) Crewe North (02/1948) Preston (09/1950) Carlisle Upperby (10/1957) Carlisle Upperby (10/1962). The locomotive was withdrawn on 3 December 1960, and cut up at Crewe Works. Known mileage in service totalled 1,259,416 (up the end of 1960).

In 1956 British Railways chose loco No 45508 to be the recipient of an experimental draughting system a move which gave the previously handsome locomotive an extremely incongruous appearance, due to the addition of a hideously shaped stove pipe chimney. From all accounts the experiment did little to increase the effectiveness of the loco's steam raising capacity but did attract almost universal condemnation from the railway fraternity. This locomotive was one of ten 'Patriot' class engines which never received names. (Unnamed 45508, 45510, 45513, 45517, 45542, 45544, 45547, 45549, 45550 and 45551)

**Many described the experimental stove pipe chimney as an act of vandalism, and the 'upturned bucket' shape certainly did nothing to improve the looks of the engine. No 45508 is pictured between duties at Crewe North depot on 25/06/1960. Note 6P above the BR cabside number. *D Forsyth/Colour Rail***

Patriot No 45508 is pictured hauling a heavy Yorkshire–Lancashire service in 1959. *Edward Talbot Collection*

No 5508 seen in original condition at Bushbury depot in 1935. Note 5XP under the LMS cabside number. *Edward Talbot Collection*

Original LMS number **6005**, 1934 LMS number **5509**, British Railways number **45509**, the locomotive was named **THE DERBYSHIRE YEOMANRY** in November 1951. The name plate incorporated a military crest.

This loco was originally allocated the name *Commando,* which was never carried. Loco No 6005, the Claughton locomotive it replaced (withdrawn September 1932) was unnamed.

Built at Crewe, the locomotive entered service on 19 August 1932 (then unnamed). Principal shed allocations for this loco included Camden (09/1935) Willesden (04/1944) Willesden (02/1948) Willesden (09/1950) Derby (10/1957) Newton Heath (08/1961). The locomotive was withdrawn on 12/08/1961, and cut up at Crewe Works. Known mileage in service totalled 1,249,852 (up the end of 1961).

The regiment was first formed as the Derbyshire Corps of Fencible Cavalry in 1794, as a regiment of full-time soldiers intended for home defensive duties. The regiment changed shortly thereafter to the Derbyshire Corps of Yeomanry Cavalry (a part-time yeomanry regiment). In 1834, the various yeomanry troops were

**This fascinating official LMS image was taken in 1939. Patriot No 5509 (then unnamed) is pictured with a rake of Southern Railway (SR) stock heading a train from the south coast north over Bushey Troughs. This locomotive was not named until November 1951 when it became BR 45509.** *David Anderson Collection*

**LMS No 5509 is pictured at Derby circa 1940. This was one of only six Patriots to remain coupled to the same tender for its entire working life.** *Mike Martin Archive/LMS-Patriot Project*

regimented as the Derbyshire Yeomanry Cavalry. The regiment sponsored two companies of the Imperial Yeomanry in 1900, for service in the South African War, and in 1901 was itself reorganized as mounted infantry as the Derbyshire Imperial Yeomanry. In 1908 it was transferred into the Territorial Force, returning to a cavalry role and equipping as dragoons, under the new title of The Derbyshire Yeomanry. During the First World War the regiment was based in the Middle East and associated with all major military actions in that region. Returning to that region in the early years of WWII the regiment fought during the battle for El Alamien as part of 4th Armoured Brigade within the 7th Armoured Division (The Desert Rats).

Original LMS number **6012**, 1934 LMS number **5510**, British Railways number **45510**, the locomotive was unnamed. Loco No 6012, the Claughton locomotive it replaced (withdrawn September 1932) was also unnamed.

Built at Crewe, the locomotive entered service on 24 August 1932. Principal shed allocations for this loco included Camden (09/1935) Willesden (04/1944) Willesden (02/1948) Crewe North (09/1950) Willesden (10/1957) Lancaster Green Ayre (06/1962). The locomotive was withdrawn on 9 June 1962, and cut up at Crewe Works. Known mileage in service totalled 1,311,573 (up to 17/06/61).

**Between turns, BR No 45510 is pictured at Camden in 1959.** *Roy Vincent/Transport Treasury*

BR No 45510 is pictured in a filthy condition at Carnforth depot 21/05/1960. K C H *Fairley/Colour Rail*

Turned and waiting to depart with an up excursion No 45510 is pictured at Llandudno in June 1963. At that time travellers from the seaside town still enjoyed the protection of an overall station roof, in modern times only a small section of that structure remains in place. *Colour Rail*

Original LMS number **5942**, 1934 LMS number **5511**, British Railways number **45511**, the locomotive was named **ISLE OF MAN** in 1938. The name plate incorporated a crest with the islands coat of arms. Loco No 5942, the Claughton locomotive it replaced (withdrawn September 1932) was unnamed.

Built at Crewe, the locomotive entered service on 31 August 1932 (then unnamed). Principal shed allocations for this loco included Camden (09/1935) Bushbury (04/1944) Crewe North (02/1948) Crewe North (09/1950) Willesden (10/1957) Carlisle Upperby (02/1962). The locomotive was withdrawn on 11 February 1962, and cut up at Crewe Works. Known mileage in service totalled 1,286,113 (up to 02/09/60).

Set in the Irish Sea the Isle of Man with its capital town of Douglas has an area of 227 square miles; it is an independent sovereign country under the crown. Once a Viking stronghold the island was annexed by England in the 13th century and is

BR No 45511 ISLE OF MAN is pictured at Euston Station on 02/06/1957 waiting to depart with the Euston-Watford Junction-Bletchley Northampton Castle leg of the R.C.T.S 'The Mercian' railtour. At Northampton the train was taken over by Stanier Black Five No 45091 for the next leg to Blisworth via Nuneaton Trent Vale and Rugby. For the final leg, Blisworth to London St Pancras, Ivatt Mogul No 43018 was rostered. *AE Bennett/Transport Treasury*

**Nameplate of No 45511, complete with the famous IOM three legged symbol.** *David Anderson*

ruled by a Lieutenant governor appointed by the crown but acting with its own parliament, the Tynwald, which has tax raising and law making powers. The highest point of the island is Snaefell (2034 feet) from where on a clear day the outlines of England, Scotland, Ireland and Wales are all visible, the mountain is served by a narrow gauge railway built in 1895. The island still has sections of a narrow gauge steam railway in operation. The Isle of Man Steam Railway once served all of the islands major centres of population but now only one line remains. Originally built in the late 1800's the 3 feet gauge lines then covered about fifty miles. Now only the southern line, operating since 1874 continues. It covers around 15 miles from Douglas to Port Erin. That section was saved by the Marquis of Ailsa, who bravely funded the continuation of the line, after competition from other forms of transport threatened the whole line with closure in the 1960's. The line was taken over by the Manx Government in the 1970's to run as a tourist attraction. With regular steamer sailings from the mainland the island developed into a popular holiday destination. The LNWR originated and the LMS continued to operate crossings between Liverpool/Fleetwood and Douglas whilst other companies operated seasonal services from Silloth to Douglas, Whitehaven to Ramsey, Barrow in Furness to Douglas, Ardrossan to Douglas and Llandudno to Douglas. In modern times the Isle of Man has connections by air with several UK airports and regular sea crossings from Liverpool and Fleetwood.

Original LMS number **5966**, 1934 LMS number **5512**, British Railways number **45512**, the locomotive was named **BUNSEN**. Loco No 5966, the Claughton locomotive it replaced (withdrawn September 1932) also carried the name Bunsen (from February 1922).

Built at Crewe, the locomotive entered service on 14 September 1932. This locomotive was rebuilt incorporation a Stanier '2A' tapered boiler, 17″ diameter cylinders, new smoke box, double chimney, new cab and larger Stanier tender re-entering service on 26 July 1948, new Royal Scot style curved and tapered smoke deflectors were later fitted. Principal shed allocations for this loco included Longsight (09/1935) Bushbury (04/1944) Crewe North (02/1948) Carlisle Upperby (09/1950) Carlisle Upperby (10/1957) Carlisle Kingmoor (02/1965). The locomotive was withdrawn on 27 March 1965, and cut up at Motherwell Machinery & Scrap Ltd, Wishaw. Known mileage in service as a 5XP/6P loco 913,914, and thereafter 670,703 as a 7P loco, which totalled 1,584,617 (up the end of 1960).

Even with the benefit of hindsight it is difficult to see how the name *Bunsen* came to be chosen by the LNWR in 1922 for a locomotive built in 1920. The name is almost certainly a direct reference to the inventor of that clever piece of laboratory equipment the gas 'Bunsen Burner'. Robert Wilhelm Bunsen (1811–1899) was born in Gottingen, Germany on 31 March 1811 and who undertook groundbreaking work in the fields of organic chemistry and spectrometry. He came to prominence during the 1830s when carrying out experiments using organic arsenic compounds. During the course of his work a laboratory explosion caused him to lose the sight of one eye and suffer a severe case of arsenic poisoning, he was by all accounts lucky to escape with his life. He invented many lab tools, including a grease-spot photometer, a galvanic battery and an ice calorimeter, and, together with a colleague Gustav Robert Kirchhoff, he developed a spectrometer (1859) that led to the discovery of the elements caesium and rubidium. Circa 1855 Bunsen had university mechanic Peter Desaga build a gas burner that would produce a steady and near-colourless flame for lab experiments (Bunsen burner).

LMS No 5966 is pictured thundering up Camden Bank with a down express in this evocative 1934 image. Not a banking engine in sight! The happy locomotive crew look keen to wave to the photographer. Note the splendid LNWR signal gantry. *Edward Talbot Collection*

BR No 45512 BUNSEN pictured in rebuilt form passing Farrington Junction with a down fitted freight in 1962, this loco was rebuilt by BR in 1948 and was one of the last to be withdrawn. Note the LMS Stanier 9 ton 4000 gallon capacity tender as fitted to the rebuilt Patriot locomotives. *M Chapman/Colour Rail*

Original LMS number **5958**, 1934 LMS number **5513**, British Railways number **45513**, the locomotive was unnamed. Loco No 5958, the Claughton locomotive it replaced (withdrawn July 1932) was also unnamed.

Built at Crewe, the locomotive entered service on 19 September 1932. Principal shed allocations for this loco included Camden (09/1935) Bushbury (04/1944) Preston (02/1948) Crewe North (09/1950) Carlisle Upperby (10/1957) Edge Hill (09/1962). The locomotive was withdrawn on 15 September 1962, and cut up at Crewe Works. Known mileage in service totalled 1,462,093 (up to the end of 1961). The highest recorded for an un-rebuilt member of the class.

**LMS No 5958 is pictured as a relatively new locomotive at Kentish Town in 1934, prior to backing down to St Pancras to head a Midland service. In this particular livery style the power classification is shown as 5X only, and is carried to the right of the window (on the narrow section of cab).** *Edward Talbot Collection*

**Unnamed BR locomotive No 45513 is pictured at speed on the West Coast Mainline (WCML) near Symington, 15/06/1960. Note the power classification 6P carried above the cabside number.** *David Anderson*

Original LMS number **5983**, 1934 LMS number **5514**, British Railways number **45514**, the locomotive was named **HOLYHEAD** in 1938. Loco No 5983, the Claughton locomotive it replaced (withdrawn October 1932) was unnamed.

Built at Crewe, the locomotive entered service on 21 September 1932. This locomotive was rebuilt incorporating a Stanier '2A' tapered boiler, 17″ diameter cylinders, new smoke box, double chimney, new cab and larger Stanier tender re-entering service on 26 March 1947, new Royal Scot style curved and tapered smoke deflectors were later fitted. Principal shed allocations for this loco included Aston (09/1935) Crewe North (04/1944) Bushbury (02/1948) Camden (09/1950) Camden (10/1957) Derby (ex Millhouses) (05/1961). The locomotive was withdrawn on 27 May 1961, and cut up at Crewe Works having the dubious distinction of being the first of the rebuilt Patriots to be taken out of service. Known mileage in service as a 5XP/6P loco 709,185, and thereafter 798,261 as a 7P loco, which totalled 1,507,446, (up to January 1961).

**BR No 45514 is pictured on the WCML in this 1960s image; this locomotive was rebuilt by British Railways in 1947 and was the first of the rebuilt engines to be withdrawn.** *Colour Rail*

Situated on Holy Island off the coast of Anglesey, the once important port of Holyhead was the western terminus of the London & North Western Railway Company, the City of Dublin Steam Packet Company and the LMSR for their cross-channel Irish passenger, freight and mail services to and from Dublin (North Wall) Kingston (Dun Laoghaire) and to the Irish port of Greenore from the terminus at Admiralty Pier. It was also the ultimate destination for the Irish Mail express service from London Euston. Historically, the Chester & Holyhead Railway was an independent railway company formed to link up with the Chester & Crewe Railway and by 1842 a through route was in operation between London and Chester with the rails then reaching Bangor in 1848. In those early days passengers travelled onto Anglesey via Telford's suspension road bridge over the Menai Straits until the Britannia tubular rail bridge opened in 1850.

**Rebuilt BR loco No 45514 is pictured double heading a Palatine express service with Jubilee 4-6-0 No 45683 HOGUE at Swinton, Manchester in 1960.** *Mike Stokes Collection*

Original LMS number **5992**, 1934 LMS number **5515**, British Railways number **45515**, the locomotive was named **CAERNARVON** in January 1939. Loco No 5992, the Claughton locomotive it replaced (withdrawn September 1932) was unnamed. The name *Caernarvon* was however previously allocated to a London & North Western Railway 'George V' class 4-4-0, No. 984.

Built at Crewe, the locomotive entered service on 27 September 1932 (unnamed). Principal shed allocations for this loco included Aston (09/1935) Preston (04/1944) Preston (02/1948) Edge Hill (09/1950) Edge Hill (10/1957) Newton Heath (06/1962). The locomotive was withdrawn on 9 June 1962, and cut up at Crewe Works. Known mileage in service totalled 1,349,670 (up to the end of 1961).

Located overlooking the southern end of the Menai Straits on the former L&NWR and LMSR line between Bangor and Pwhelli lays the historically important town of Caernarvon. This popular resort is famous for its well preserved and imposing castle, the foundation stone of which was laid in 1283. In 1969 it was the spectacular setting for the investiture of Prince Charles as the Prince of Wales. Although no longer main line railway connected the town has in recent times become an important 'railway' location as the western terminus of the well patronised preserved narrow gauge Welsh Highland Railway sits snugly below the towering ramparts of the ancient castle. A comprehensive, and mainly steam hauled, service operates between the town and Porthmadog via Snowdonia, and connects with the Ffestiniog Steam Railway.

**Reminisent of the time BR No 45515, although still a handsome looking engine, is in need of a clean in this picture taken at Manchester Exchange station, 08/05/1961. *D Forsyth/Colour Rail***

Original LMS number **5982**, 1934 LMS number **5516**, British Railways number **45516**, the locomotive was named **THE BEDFORDSHIRE AND HERTFORDSHIRE REGIMENT** in 1938. Comprised of 39 letters this was the longest name of any locomotive in the class and a regimental crest was carried above the name plate. Loco No 5982, the Claughton locomotive it replaced (withdrawn October 1932) was unnamed.

Built at Crewe, the locomotive entered service on 10 October 1932 (unnamed). Principal shed allocations for this loco included Patricroft (09/1935) Preston (04/1944) Preston (02/1948) Edge Hill (09/1950) Edge Hill (10/1957) Warrington (Dallam) (06/1961). The locomotive was withdrawn on 22 July 1961, and cut up at Crewe Works. Known mileage in service totalled 1,330,544 (up to the end of 1961).

The regiment was known as the Bedfordshire Regiment until after World War 1 and was an infantry regiment originally formed in 1881 from other historically significant corps of military. That regiment had a truly illustrious past and served in theatres of war and trouble spots throughout the former British Empire and beyond, including seeing action in the Nine Years War, the War of Spanish Succession and the American War of Independence. On 29 July 1919 the regiment was renamed as the Bedfordshire and Hertfordshire Regiment in recognition of the huge contribution made during the Great War by men recruited from the county of Hertfordshire. The regiment was in 1925 awarded in excess of 70 honours for service in the Great War and in 1957 some 18 Second World War honours were additionally bestowed upon the regiment. Following the later reorganisation of the British Army the Bedfordshire and Hertfordshire Regiment became part of the East Anglian Regiment.

BR No 45516 THE BEDFORDSHIRE AND HERTFORDSHIRE REGIMENT stands outside the erecting shop at Crewe Works. This loco at that time carried an unusual livery, BR numbers on LMS maroon paint. The loco was at 'the works' between 17/01/49 and 09/02/49 for heavy intermediate examination/repairs. Note the 5XP power rating under the BR cabside number also a chalk written note on the cab informs interested parties that the locos boiler has been filled with water. *Edward Talbot Collection*

On 17/02/50 No 45516 worked a special troop train from Southampton Docks hauling members of the 1st Battalion of the regiment after which it was named. A group of officers are pictured with the loco prior to its departure. *David Anderson Collection*

No 45516 is pictured at Cheadle Hulme station on 13/08/60. There is no sign of the fireman, so we can assume that he was 'bending his back' at the time whilst the driver's main focus of attention during the station stop appears to be his brew can! Note the BR 6P power classification above the number on the cabside. *D Forsyth/ Colour Rail*

Original LMS number **5952**, 1934 LMS number **5517**, British Railways number **45517**, the locomotive was unnamed. Loco No 5952, the Claughton locomotive it replaced (withdrawn November 1932) was also unnamed.

Built at Crewe, the locomotive entered service on 6 February 1933. Principal shed allocations for this loco included Longsight (09/1935) Crewe North (04/1944) Edge Hill (02/1948) Carlisle Upperby (09/1950) Willesden (10/1957) Bank Hall (06/1962). The locomotive was withdrawn on 9 June 1962, and cut up at Crewe Works. Known mileage in service totalled 1,295,802 (up to the end of 1960).

**BR No 45517 is pictured at speed passing Crawford on the WCML in July 1960 with a Glasgow Central to Blackpool North relief excursion.** *David Anderson*

No 45517 is pictured at Bolton Station on 05/08/61, with a Manchester train. The loco had by this time been fitted with AWS equipment, the battery box for which can be seen against the cab body towards the rear of the running plate. *D Forsyth/Colour Rail*

No 45517 is pictured leaving York shortly after being renumbered as a BR loco on 12/05/48. *Colour Rail*

**BR No 45518 BRADSHAW is pictured with the up Mancunian on Castlethorpe Troughs, with 12 coaches the 5XP/6P is working hard, August 1958.** *T B Owen/LMS-Patriot Project*

Original LMS number **6006**, 1934 LMS number **5518**, British Railways number **45518**, the locomotive was named **BRADSHAW** in 1939. Loco No 6006, the Claughton locomotive it replaced (withdrawn November 1932) was unnamed.

Built at Crewe, the locomotive entered service on 20 February 1933 (then unnamed). Principal shed allocations for this loco included Camden (09/1935) Willesden (04/1944) Carlisle Upperby (02/1948) Carlisle Upperby (09/1950) Edge Hill (10/1957) Lancaster Green Ayre (10/1962). The locomotive was withdrawn on 3 November 1962, and cut up at Crewe Works. Known mileage in service totalled 1,316,939 (up 19/09/61).

The name Bradshaw, which has long been associated with railway travel and railway time tables, has been brought to prominence post millennium by the BBC Television series Great British Railway Journeys. In which, using a venerable Bradshaw publication the presenter navigated a series of rail journeys around the UK in an attempt to trace the footsteps of Victorian traveller, publisher, cartographer and printer George Bradshaw (1801-1853). Having been educated at Pendleton near Salford, Bradshaw became apprenticed to a Manchester engineer called Beale. He moved to work in Belfast in 1820 and in 1822 returned to Manchester to set up his own company with the purpose of producing engravings from which detailed maps were made. Bradshaw was a deeply religious man and in his adult life he joined the Society of Friends (Quakers) thereafter devoting a great deal of his time to philanthropic work. Following Quakers beliefs the Bradshaw guides avoided the use of months or day names of Roman deities (i.e. perceived Pagan beliefs) and so January for example was written as 'First Month' and February as 'Second Month' etc accordingly days of the week were shown as Monday 'First Day' etc. Having already published Bradshaw's Maps of Inland Navigation he produced his first compilation of railway timetables in 1839. As the popularity and use of the railways increased Bradshaw's company prospered with his guide becoming a monthly publication, a continental version was also produced. In 1853 Bradshaw contracted cholera whilst touring Norway and died in the September of that year, he is buried in the cemetery adjoining Oslo Cathedral. In 1934 the company set up by George Bradshaw also began publishing a guide to the major airline routes both within Europe and those transcontinental flights that originated from Europe and the UK. The last edition of his railway guide, No 1521 was dated May 1961. The publication used in the BBC TV series is in fact a Bradshaw's Tourist Handbook (circa 1860) not a Bradshaw's Timetable compilation.

BR No 45518 is pictured at Crewe North depot in 1948 when recently renumbered note also the 5XP power classification carried midway between the new number and the cab window, however at that time the locomotives's tender was still lettered LMS. *Mike Stokes Collection*

In this 1960s image No 45518 is seen at Hellifield with an up passenger service. *M Chapman/Colour Rail*

Original LMS number **6008**, 1934 LMS number **5519**, British Railways number **45519**, the locomotive was named **LADY GODIVA** in 1939. Loco No 6008, the Claughton locomotive it replaced (withdrawn December 1932) was also named *Lady Godiva* from 05/1923).

Built at Crewe, the locomotive entered service on 25 February 1933. Principal shed allocations for this loco included Edge Hill (09/1935) Willesden (04/1944) Preston (02/1948) Preston (09/1950) Longsight (10/1957) Bristol Barrow Road (03/1962). The locomotive was withdrawn on 17 March 1962, and cut up at Crewe Works. Known mileage in service totalled 1,331,133 (up to 12/03/60).

Perhaps Coventry's most famous sister was the Anglo Saxon gentlewomen Godiva (aka Godgifu) who reputedly rode naked on horseback through that Mercian city in the 11th century. She was the wife of Leofric who, as the Earl of Mercia, was one of Britain's most powerful noblemen. However history is unclear as to whether the aforementioned lady was actually 'the Godiva' who made the infamous naked ride. Leofric died in 1057 and Godiva is mentioned in the Doomsday Book of 1086 as being the beneficiary of all his lands and estates, which included Coventry (she would almost certainly have been dead herself by that time). According to legend the good lady persistently tried to persuade her husband to reduce the taxes levied upon the people of Coventry. Leofric was so exasperated with her constant complaining that he eventually struck a deal with her. He stated that if she would ride naked through the busy market place he would reduce the taxes. She did so with only a shock of her long hair to cover her modesty, reportedly Leofric kept his word. Further additions to the amusing tale suggested that Godiva's husband banned all persons from looking at her during the ride and the one man who peeped was struck blind hence 'Peeping Tom'.

Climbing the famous Lickey Incline with a down train, BR No 45519 is pictured hard at work in this 1960s image.
*Colour Rail*

Original LMS number **5954**, 1934 LMS number **5520**, British Railways number **45520**, the locomotive was named **LLANDUDNO** in 1937, and a civic crest was carried above the nameplate. Loco No 5954, the Claughton locomotive it replaced (withdrawn December 1932) was unnamed.

Built at Derby, the locomotive entered service on 17 February 1933 (then unnamed). Principal shed allocations for this loco included Edge Hill (09/1935) Edge Hill (04/1944) Edge Hill (02/1948) Longsight (09/1950) Longsight (10/1957) Edge Hill (05/1962). The locomotive was withdrawn on 19 May 1962, and cut up at Crewe Works. Known mileage in service totalled 1,359,575 (up to the end of 1961).

Llandudno with its sweeping bay has long been one of the most popular Welsh coast holiday destinations, which at one time even enjoyed summer steamer sailings to the Isle of Man. North Shore beach is enclosed by the headlands of Great Orme (679 feet) which is reached by cable operated tramway and Little Orme (464 feet). The imposing West Shore beach affords visitors commanding views of the Conway Estuary and Snowdonia. Served by the main coastal railway from 1858, the resort is only a short journey time from the conurbations of Liverpool and Manchester making it a convenient journey for both holidaymakers and city commuters alike. By 1885, the town's population had risen to over 5,000, a figure which then doubled by the turn of the century and in modern times has risen to a little over 20,000. Due to the popularity of railway communication, the town was provided with business trains which included 'club' coaches introduced by the L&NWR from 1908 and thereafter continued by the LMSR, and to a lesser degree by BR.

LMS No 5954 as a newly introduced loco is pictured at Kentish Town in April 1933. *Edward Talbot Collection*

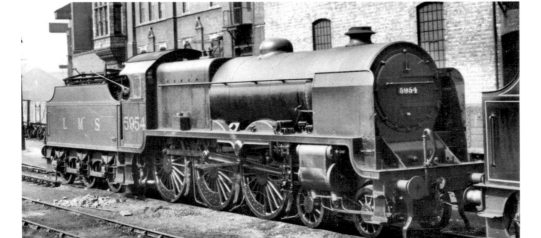

LMS No 5520 is pictured resplendent in Crimson Lake lined livery at Crewe North depot in 1936, then unnamed. In this instance the 5XP power rating is shown on the narrow strip adjacent to the window with '5X' on one line and the 'P' centred underneath it. *Edward Talbot Collection*

BR NO 45520 is seen at speed passing Cheadle Hulme signal box in 1960. *Mike Stokes Collection*

Original LMS number **5933**, 1934 LMS number **5521**, British Railways number **45521**, the locomotive was named **RHYL** in 1937 and a civic crest was carried above the nameplate. This locomotive shares with Patriot No 45528 R.E.M.E. the distinction of having the shortest name. Loco No 5933, the Claughton locomotive it replaced (withdrawn December 1932) was unnamed.

Built at Derby, the locomotive entered service on 4 March 1933 (then unnamed). This locomotive was rebuilt incorporation a Stanier '2A' tapered boiler, 17″ diameter cylinders, new smoke box, double chimney, new cab and larger Stanier tender re-entering service on 31/10/1946, new Royal Scot style curved and tapered smoke deflectors were later fitted. Principal shed allocations for this loco included Edge Hill (09/1935) Crewe North (04/1944) Edge Hill (02/1948) Warrington (09/1950) Edge Hill (10/1957) Wigan Springs Branch (09/1963). The locomotive was withdrawn on 28 September 1963, and cut up at Crewe Works. Available data for 'miles in service' not known. Known mileage in service as a 5XP/6P loco 674,593, and thereafter 928,635 as a 7P loco, which totalled 1,603,228, (during the life of the loco).

**LMS No 5521 RHYL looks superb in original LMS livery as she prepares to depart from Birmingham New Street station on 17/05/38. Note that in this instance the 5XP power classification is carried in the more usual place above the cabside number.** *Edward Talbot Collection*

LMS 5521 is pictured at Camden depot 'as rebuilt' in December 1936 and before the addition of smoke deflectors. The power rating is shown as 6P (reclassified by BR as 7P 1951) but in this instance is below the cabside number. *Colour Rail*

BR No 45521 RHYL in rebuilt form and with smoke deflectors is pictured at London Euston station in this 1960 image, having recently arrived from Liverpool Lime Street with The Merseyside Express. *Colour Rail*

**BR No 45521 is pictured being serviced (and prior to turning) at Morecambe depot in June 1963, note the grimy condition of the loco when compared with images taken earlier.** *Keith Langston*

Sandy beaches and holiday entertainment at Rhyl and its eastern neighbour Prestatyn produced a healthy financial return for the L&NWR and LMSR companies, the railway helping to open up passenger travel along the North Wales coast with extra trains and excursion traffic from the main centres of Lancashire, Yorkshire, Merseyside and the Midlands. Visitors could visit the nearby Rhuddlan Castle, dating from 1277 and also a miniature railway engineered by Bassett–Lowke and Henry Greenly, which operated on tracks laid around the shore of the towns Marine Lake, adjacent to the towns harbour and alongside the Welsh Coast mainline.

**Patriot 5521 (original LMS number) is pictured prior to 1037 with what is thought to be a Blackpool service although the location is a mystery? Note the 'enthusiast' on the embankment.** *Edward Talbot Collection*

Original LMS number **5973**, 1934 LMS number **5522**, British Railways number **45522**, the locomotive was named **PRESTATYN** in 1939 and a civic crest was carried above the nameplate. Loco No 5973, the Claughton locomotive it replaced (withdrawn December 1932) was unnamed.

Built at Derby, the locomotive entered service on 3 March 1933 (then unnamed). This locomotive was rebuilt incorporation a Stanier '2A' tapered boiler, 17″ diameter cylinders, new smoke box, double chimney, new cab and larger Stanier tender in re-entering service on 7 February 1949, new Royal Scot style curved and tapered smoke deflectors were later fitted. Principal shed allocations for this loco included Bushbury (09/1935) Crewe North (04/1944) Crewe North (02/1948) Camden (09/1950) Camden (10/1957) Longsight (09/1964). The locomotive was withdrawn on 19 September 1964, and cut up at Central Wagon

**LMS No 5522 (then still unnamed) is pictured at Gaydon Loops on the WCML with an up express train on 28/08/37.** *Edward Talbot Collection*

Co. Ince, Wigan. Known mileage, in service as a 5XP/6P loco 823,445, and thereafter 716,561, as a 7P loco, which totalled 1,603,228 (up to 11/02/61).

Prestatyn is often referred to as the gateway to the North Wales coastal area, and it is the most easterly of the beautiful North Wales coastal resorts. The Town Centre is nestled between magnificent sandy beaches and a spectacular hillside, where mountain air meets salty sea breezes. Uniquely situated with its 'shield' of hills and mountains, Prestatyn is said to boast a distinctly favourable micro climate all of its own. Prestatyn is famous for its sunny sands and coastline with rolling dunes, but is also considered as the northern gateway for walking in North Wales. It not only boasts the start (or end) of the Offa's Dyke National Trail but also features the North Wales Path, Clwydian Way and Dee Way. The area is rich in history and the surrounding countryside offers walks in areas of outstanding natural beauty, and a nearby nature reserve is designated a Site of Special Scientific Interest (SSSI).

**Rebuilt Patriot BR number 45522 PRESTATYN is pictured leaving Dore and Totley in July 1964. The locomotive which had then only a matter of weeks left in service is in a filthy condition and had by that time lost its nameplate (although the backing plate can be seen).** *Keith Langston Collection*

Original LMS number **6026**, 1934 LMS number **5523**, British Railways number **45523**, the locomotive was named **BANGOR** in 1939. Loco No 6026, the Claughton locomotive it replaced (withdrawn December 1932) was unnamed.

Built at Crewe, the locomotive entered service on 8 March 1933 (then unnamed). This locomotive was rebuilt incorporation a Stanier '2A' tapered boiler, 17″ diameter cylinders, new smoke box, double chimney, new cab and larger Stanier tender re-entering service on 8 October 1948, new Royal Scot style curved and tapered smoke deflectors were later fitted. Principal shed allocations for this loco included Bushbury (09/1935) Crewe North (04/1944) Edge Hill (02/1948) Crewe North (09/1950) Camden (10/1957) Willesden (01/1964). The locomotive was withdrawn on 25 January 1964, and cut up at Crewe Works. Known mileage in service as a 5XP/6P loco 791,994, and thereafter 701,596, as a 7P loco, which totalled 1,493,590 (up to 15/06/61).

Bangor is a historic cathedral and university city in North Wales and is situated on the Menai Straits overlooking the Menai Bridge and the Isle of Anglesey, the busy town is located 9 miles to the north east of Caernarvon. Bangor has a proud history which can be traced back to 525 AD when Deiniol, a Celtic missionary,

BR rebuilt Patriot No 45523 BANGOR is pictured under the coaling stage at Crewe North depot on 25/06/60. *D Forsyth/Colour Rail*

established a monastic community on the site of the present cathedral. For centuries it remained a small town of two streets, with the cathedral as its focal point, and few positive signs of expansion. The town developed along with the nearby slate industry and became even more important when the building of Thomas Telford's coach road and suspension bridge placed it directly on the main London to Holyhead route (now A5). In 1822 a steam packet service was introduced between the then steadily growing town and the city of Liverpool. The, now world famous, university was founded in 1884. Preserved transport artefacts in the collection at nearby Penrhyn Castle (building completed in 1840) include an interesting display of early steam locomotives.

**LMS No 5523 is pictured departing from Lancaster with a WCML down train in 1938 (then unnamed).** *Colour Rail*

LMS No 5523 is pictured between turns (and before being named) at Crewe North depot circa 1938. *Mike Martin Collection*

Rebuilt Patriot No 45523 BANGOR gets away smartly from Lichfield with a down WCML express service in June 1956. Colour Rail

Original LMS number **5907**, 1934 LMS number **5524**, British Railways number **45524**, the locomotive was named **SIR FREDERICK HARRISON** (1933) and then renamed **BLACKPOOL** in 1937 in a ceremony at the town's station on 23 March 1936 in the presence of Sir Josiah Stamp, the Chairman of the LMSR. Loco No 5907, the Claughton locomotive it replaced (withdrawn January 1933) was also named Sir Frederick Harrison.

Built at Crewe, the locomotive entered service on 14 March 1933. Principal shed allocations for this loco included Patricroft (09/1935) Preston (04/1944) Preston (02/1948) Bushbury (09/1950) Carlisle Upperby (10/1957) Edge Hill (09/1962). No 5524 (later No.45524) regularly worked the 'Fylde Coast Express' between London Euston and Blackpool in 4 hours 22 minutes, a timing which was 47 minutes faster than the pre-Grouping company schedule. The locomotive was withdrawn on 15 September 1962, and cut up at Crewe Works. Known mileage in service totalled 1,272,536 (up to 11/04/61).

The North West of England Blackpool began to develop as a recreational resort in the mid-18th century and became busiest during the summer months when the Lancashire and Yorkshire mines, factories and mills closed down for the annual 'wakes' or holidays. At first reached by a branch line of the Preston & Wyre Railway, its seven mile promenade and three piers are well-known for the autumn illuminations, the seafront vista being dominated by the 518 feet-high Blackpool

LMS No 5524 is pictured on shed at Crewe post 1937; the loco carries the name BLACKPOOL and is seen prior to passing into BR ownership. *Edward Talbot Collection*

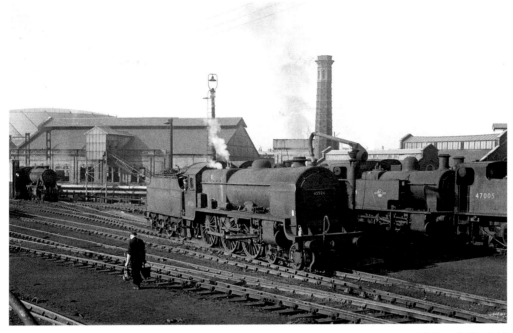

BR No 45524 is pictured on the BR LMR depot at Birkenhead in this 1960s image. The plume of steam to the right of the large chimney indicates the location of the ex GWR depot, note also the dock shunters on the road beyond the Patriot. *Colour Rail*

A typical 1960s scene, a locomotive crew change is taking place at Carlisle; BR No 45524 is set to depart with an up express service. *D Forsyth/Colour Rail*

Tower. Blackpool's success owes much to the railway and the additional popularity of an extensive electric tramway system. The lines serving Blackpool were jointly owned by the Lancashire & Yorkshire and the London & North Western Railways, their termini becoming Blackpool (Talbot Road) (later North) and Central. The former station was rebuilt with 15 platforms in 1898 and in 1900, Central station with 14 platforms. By 1903, the original coast line from Lytham was bypassed by a direct line from Kirkham, this allowing a faster running time and a five-mile reduction in distance from Preston. In 1919, a total of 413,000 passengers arrived at Blackpool at the height of the summer season and on a Saturday in August 1935; a remarkable number of 467 trains arrived and departed from the resort's two stations. The advent of motor transport affected passenger traffic on the once-important railways with the closure of Central station and the termination of the coast line at Blackpool (South) in 1964. Main line services were concentrated at Blackpool (North) after the closure of the direct line in 1967, the station being rebuilt in 1974.

**Patriot No 45524 BLACKPOOL is pictured outside Crewe Works in 1959.** *F Forsyth/Colour Rail*

Original LMS number **5916**, 1934 LMS number **5525**, British Railways number **45525**, the locomotive was named **E. TOOTAL BROADHURST** (1933) and then renamed **COLWYN BAY** in 1937 and dedicated during a ceremony at the town's station on 16 June 1938, a civic crest was carried above the nameplate. Loco No 5916, the Claughton locomotive it replaced (withdrawn November 1932) was also named *E. Tootal Broadhurst* (the name was later bestowed on loco No 5534 (45534)*.

Built at Derby, the locomotive entered service on 22 March 1933. This locomotive was rebuilt incorporation a Stanier '2A' tapered boiler, 17″ diameter cylinders, new smoke box, double chimney, new cab and larger Stanier tender re-entering service on 20 August 1948, new Royal Scot style curved and tapered smoke deflectors were later fitted. Principal shed allocations for this loco included Bushbury (09/1935) Edge Hill (04/1944) Edge Hill (02/1948) Carlisle Upperby (09/1950) Edge Hill (10/1957) Llandudno Junction (05/1963). The locomotive was withdrawn on 11 May 1963, and cut up at Crewe Works. Known mileage, in service as a 5XP/6P loco 732,736 and thereafter 737,217, as a 7P loco, which totalled 1,469,953 (up to 15/05/63).

Situated three miles to the east of Llandudno, Colwyn which was renamed Colwyn Bay in 1876, provides good holiday resort facilities. Its three mile long Victorian promenade (complete with pier) which links the town with Rhos on Sea and Penrhyn Bay has long been extremely popular with walkers and cyclists. The station, once served by LNWR services from Chester (London), and thereafter LMSR trains is still a busy transport interchange in modern times. Within an easy walk from the town is the Nant-y-Glyn Valley said to be one of the hidden gems of

LMS 5525 is seen at Crewe Works but after being refurbished and re-named COLWYN BAY in May 1938. *Mike Bentley Collection*

LMS No 5916 named E TOOTAL BROADHURST is pictured at Derby when six months old, 15/10/33. *Mike Bentley Collection*

LMS No 5525 (still named E TOOTAL BROADHURST) is pictured outside Crewe Works in 1936; note that the rods have been removed to facilitate repairs. *Mike Bentley Collection*

Rebuilt Patriot BR No 45525 COLWYN BAY re-entered service in August 1948, the loco is seen without smoke deflectors heading a down express near to Watford in November 1949. *J C Flemons/Transport Treasury*

the area. The town is close to the ancient walled town of Conwy (a World Heritage Site). Colwyn Bay is often described as being the gateway to Snowdonia, the nearby Conwy estuary and valley. Local legend has it that in 1170 Madoc, Prince of Snowdon set sail with a fleet of ships from Penrhyn Bay and actually discovered America, many years before Christopher Columbus did! The possibility that Madoc landed on the shores of Mobile Bay in 1170 AD presents a fascinating conundrum for modern day Welsh historians to unravel.

BR rebuilt loco No 45525 is pictured leaving London Euston station in September 1964. *J Flint/Transport Treasury*

BR No 45525 is pictured between turns at Patricroft, Manchester on 07/10/61. *Mike Bentley Collection*

Original LMS number **5963**, 1934 LMS number **5526**, British Railways number **45526**, the locomotive was named **MORECAMBE AND HEYSHAM** on 6 October 1937 in a ceremony at the town's station, and a civic crest was carried above the nameplate. Loco No 5963, the Claughton locomotive it replaced (withdrawn November 1932) was unnamed.

Built at Derby, the locomotive entered service on 22 March 1933 (then unnamed). This locomotive was rebuilt incorporation a Stanier '2A' tapered boiler, 17″ diameter cylinders, new smoke box, double chimney, new cab and larger Stanier tender re-entering into service on 20 August 1948, new Royal Scot style curved and tapered smoke deflectors were later fitted. Principal shed allocations for this loco included Bushbury (09/1935) Edge Hill (04/1944) Edge Hill (02/1948) Carlisle Upperby (09/1950) Carlisle Upperby (10/1957) Carlisle Upperby (05/1963). The locomotive was withdrawn on 24 October 1964, and cut up at McLellan's, Langloan. Known mileage, in service as a 5XP/6P loco 701,537, and thereafter 788,537, as a 7P loco, which totalled 1490,219, (up to 17/02/61).

Two old established Lancashire villages were merged to become known as Morecambe and Heysham and together grew to become a popular coastal holiday resort. In fact in 1889 the villages of Bare, Poulton-le-Sands and Torrisholme collectively became known as Morecambe, and those areas are still often referred

**BR rebuilt Patriot No 45526 MORECAMBE AND HEYSHAM is seen waiting to depart with a down train at Carlisle station on 26/09/59. *D Forsyth/Colour Rail***

to by their original names. Morecambe station was originally called Poulton-le-Sands, and was reached by railway from Lancaster in June 1848. By 1850, the Midland and L&NWR companies had jointly completed a through route from Leeds and Bradford to Morecambe via Keighley, Skipton and Lancaster and in the early days due to the popularity of the area there was also a direct service from London King's Cross. In 1864, a

Nameplate carried in BR service by No 45526. *David Anderson*

short branch line was opened to Morecambe from the West Coast main line at Hest Bank and by 1888 the town's two stations were renamed Euston Road and Promenade. By 1908, an electric train service was in operation serving Morecambe and Heysham from Lancaster. Railway-owned steamship sailings operated following the development of the port of Heysham to Ireland and the Isle of Man. The modern port is still an important ferry terminal for both passenger and freight sailings.

BR No 45526 is pictured at 1.12pm on 23/07/60 with a Euston -Glasgow service passing Bourne End signal box WCML. *P Pescod/Transport Treasury*

Original LMS number **5944**, 1934 LMS number **5527**, British Railways number **45527**, the locomotive was named **SOUTHPORT** and a civic crest is carried above the name plate. Loco No 5944, the Claughton locomotive it replaced (withdrawn February 1932) was unnamed.

Built at Derby, the locomotive entered service on 27 March 1933 (then unnamed). This locomotive was rebuilt incorporation a Stanier '2A' tapered boiler, 17″ diameter cylinders, new smoke box, double chimney, new cab and larger Stanier tender re-entering service on 13 September 1948, new Royal Scot style curved and tapered smoke deflectors were later fitted. Principal shed allocations for this loco included Edge Hill (09/1935) Edge Hill (04/1944) Edge Hill (02/1948) Edge Hill (09/1950) Edge Hill (10/1957) Carlisle Kingmoor (12/1964). The locomotive was withdrawn on 5 December 1964, and cut up at Arnott Young, Troon. Known mileage, in service as a 5XP/6P loco 773,199, and thereafter 737,106, as a 7P loco, which totalled 1,510,305, (during the life of the loco).

Located on the Lancashire coast within easy reach of the city of Liverpool and ten miles from Blackpool, the resort of Southport is revered as a typical Victorian seaside town and is well known for Lord Street, its broad tree-lined mile-long shopping boulevard. The town was reached by the railway on 24 July 1848 from Waterloo, Liverpool, later trains serving Southport from Liverpool Exchange

**LMS No 5527 SOUTHPORT is pictured outside Crewe Works on 12/06/38. Note the loco number is marked on various components (specifically the smoke deflector) prior to the removal of parts in order to facilitate planed painting and repair.** *Edward Talbot Collection*

Rebuilt Patriot BR No 45527 is pictured departing Carlisle with a down train on 24/08/64. *Colour Rail*

station, and a line from Manchester followed in 1855 to the London & Yorkshire Railway terminus at Chapel Street. The Cheshire Lines Committee also opened a line to a terminus at Lord Street in 1882. Later, many of the lines in the area were electrified. The intricate network of lines around Southport has now been greatly reduced, but the town retains its prosperity being not only an extremely pleasant place but also within easy commuting distance of Liverpool. The town is adjacent to Royal Birkdale Golf Club and therefore has become synonymous with world class golf events. There are a further five championship courses within a 15 minute drive of the town. The nearby 34 acre Victoria Park annually hosts the world famous Southport Flower Show.

LMS No 5527 is pictured passing Gaydon Loops, WCML with an up excursion to the Radio Olympia exhibition in London on 28/08/37. *Edward Talbot Collection*

Original LMS number **5996**, 1934 LMS number **5528**, British Railways number **45528**, the locomotive was named **R.E.M.E.**, in September 1959 .Loco No 5944, the Claughton locomotive it replaced (withdrawn February 1932) was unnamed.

Built at Derby, the locomotive entered service on 4 April 1933 (then unnamed). This locomotive was rebuilt incorporation a Stanier '2A' tapered boiler, 17″ diameter cylinders, new smoke box, double chimney, new cab and larger Stanier tender re-entering service on 27 August 1947, new Royal Scot style curved and tapered smoke deflectors were later fitted. Principal shed allocations for this loco included Polmadie (09/1935) Patricroft (04/1944) Bushbury (02/1948) Crewe North (09/1950) Crewe North (10/1957) Willesden (01/1963). The locomotive was withdrawn on 19 January 1963, and cut up at Crewe Works. Known mileage in service as a 5XP/6P loco 735,880, and thereafter 737,106 as a 7P loco, which totalled 1,472,986,(up to 26/08/61).

R.E.M.E. Royal Corps Electrical and Mechanical Engineers was formed during the Second World War. Following the findings of a review into the British army's employment of technical manpower by Sir William Beveridge the war cabinet decided that a specialist engineering regiment was an essential requisite of modern

BR rebuilt Patriot No 45528 R.E.M.E. is pictured at Willesden depot in 1962. All of the other taper-boiler Patriots bore names at the time of their rebuild; however No 45528 did not, it being named some 12 years later in 1959. *Colour Rail*

warfare. R.E.M.E. thus came into being on 1 October 1942. The first of many crucially important actions for the new regiment was to provide engineering support to the troops engaged in the famous Battle of El Alamein. R.E.M.E. has played a vital role in all of the British army's operations, being present in Palestine, Korea, Kenya, Malaya, Suez, Cyprus, Northern Ireland, the Falklands, Afghanistan and both Gulf Wars. It has also been involved in peacekeeping duties all over the globe, from the Balkans to Sierra Leone and including the former republic of Yugoslavia. R.E.M.E. has been a 'Royal' corps since its formation. Interestingly a R.E.M.E. major set up the VW factory in occupied Germany after WWII, a factory which produced the famous 'Beetle' design. The regiments motto is 'Art et Marte' which translates as 'By Skill and by Fighting'.

**BR No 45528 is pictured on 26/09/1959 waiting to depart from Carlisle with a down train.** *D Forsyth/Colour Rail*

Original LMS number **5926**, 1934 LMS number **5529**, British Railways number **45529**, the locomotive was named **SIR HERBERT WALKER K.C.B.** until 1937 and renamed **STEPHENSON** in July 1948 .Loco No 5926, the Claughton locomotive it replaced (withdrawn January 1933) was also named SIR HERBERT WALKER and the name was later carried by Patriot loco No 5535 (45535).

Built at Crewe, the locomotive entered service on 6 April 1933. This locomotive was rebuilt incorporation a Stanier '2A' tapered boiler, 17″ diameter cylinders, new smoke box, double chimney, new cab and larger Stanier tender re-entering service on 5 July 1947, new Royal Scot style curved and tapered smoke deflectors were later fitted. Principal shed allocations for this loco included Patricroft (09/1935) Edge Hill (04/1944) Bushbury (02/1948) Crewe North (09/1950) Crewe North (10/1957) Annesley (02/1964). The locomotive was withdrawn in February 1964, and cut up at Crewe Works. Known mileage in service as a 5XP/6P loco 715,897, and thereafter 834,479 as a 7P loco, which totalled 1,550,376 (end of 1963).

The name *Stephenson* bestowed in July 1948 commemorates perhaps the world's most famous locomotive and railway building family name. George Stephenson (1781-1848) was the son of a colliery steam engine keeper and was born in the Northumbrian Tyneside village of Wylam and he is often referred to as 'Father of the Railways'. Stephenson became the chief engineer in charge of the Stockton and

LMS No 5529 SIR HERBERT WALKER K.C.B. is pictured at Llandudno Junction in August 1936. *Colour Rail*

**LMS No 5529 is pictured at Preston depot in 1940, the loco is un-named but the backing plate is still in position.** *Mike Martin Collection*

**BR rebuilt Patriot No 45529 STEPHENSON is pictured heading an up relief express at Denbigh Hall, Bletchley on 27/07/63.** *David Anderson*

Darlington Railway which opened in 1825 and a year later he became engineer for the Liverpool–Manchester Railway. At that time George Stephenson joined his son Robert and engineer Timothy Hackworth in an enterprise which became a very productive business partnership, the company of Robert Stephenson & Co was formed at premises on Forth Street Newcastle. Robert Stephenson (1803–1859).

Original LMS number **6022**, 1934 LMS number **5530**, British Railways number **45530**, the locomotive was named **SIR FRANK REE** in 1937. That name was originally carried by Patriot loco (5902) No 5531 (45530). Loco No 6022 the Claughton locomotive it replaced (withdrawn January 1933) was unnamed. This locomotive was the last member of the class in BR service.

Built at Crewe, the locomotive entered service on 3 April 1933 (then unnamed). This locomotive was rebuilt incorporation a Stanier '2A' tapered boiler, 17″ diameter cylinders, new smoke box, double chimney, new cab and larger Stanier tender re-entering service on 19 October 1946, new Royal Scot style curved and tapered smoke deflectors were later fitted. Principal shed allocations for this loco included Patricroft (09/1935) Crewe North (04/1944) Longsight (02/1948) Longsight (09/1950) Longsight (10/1957) Carlisle Kingmoor (12/1965). The locomotive was withdrawn on 1 January 1965, and cut up at Motherwell Machinery & Scrap, Wishaw. Known mileage in service as a 5XP/6P loco 758,097 and thereafter 951,922 as a 7P loco, which totalled 1,710.019 (up to the end of 1963).

Sir Frank Ree was General Manager of the London & North Western Railway (LNWR) from 1909 to 1914. The name *Sir Frank Ree* was an original LNWR Claughton name carried by the loco No 1191 which later became LMS No 5902.

**LMS No 5530 SIR FRANK REE is pictured at Crewe North depot in 1937, the loco is in ex works condition and carries the 5XP power classification just below the cabside window. That name was originally carried by Patriot No 5501 from build its date until 1937, when that loco became ST. DUNSTANS.** *Mike Stokes Collection*

LMS No 5530 when newly rebuilt and without smoke deflectors (October 1946) is pictured in this official LMS photograph. The rebuilt Patriot locos incorporated a Stanier '2A' tapered boiler, 17″ diameter cylinders, new smoke box, double chimney, new cab and 3 axle Stanier 9 ton/4000 gallon tender *David Anderson Collection*

It was not uncommon to see rebuilt Patriot locomotives on duty with the London St. Pancras-Manchester Central express service named The Palatine, the London departure time was 7.55am with the return service timed to leave Manchester at 2.25pm. Rebuilt BR Patriot No 45530 SIR FRANK REE is pictured in 1962 waiting to work the up service. *D Forsyth/Colour Rail*

No 45530 is pictured at Willesden depot on 07/05/64, and although it is some 18 months prior to withdrawal the loco has already lost its nameplates, although the backing plates remain. Note electric overhead power cable warning flashes affixed to the firebox, boiler and smoke deflector. *Keith Langston*

Original LMS number **6027**, 1934 LMS number **5531**, British Railways number **45531**, the locomotive was named **SIR FREDERICK HARRISON** in 1937. Loco No 6027 the Claughton locomotive it replaced (withdrawn January 1933) was unnamed. This name was also carried by LNWR Claughton class loco No 1319 (LMS 5907) until January 1933 and thereafter by Patriot No 5524 (which was renamed BLACKPOOL).

Built at Crewe, the locomotive entered service on 7 April 1933 (then unnamed). This locomotive was rebuilt incorporation a Stanier '2A' tapered boiler, 17″ diameter cylinders, new smoke box, double chimney, new cab and larger Stanier tender re-entering service on 13 December 1947, new Royal Scot style curved and tapered smoke deflectors were later fitted. Principal shed allocations for this loco included Camden (09/1935) Camden (04/1944) Bushbury (02/1948) Edge Hill (09/1950) Edge Hill (10/1957) Carlisle Kingmoor (10/1965). The locomotive was withdrawn on 30 October 1965, and cut up at Campbell's, Airdrie. Known mileage in service as a 5XP/6P loco 839,288 and thereafter 759,870 as a 7P loco, which totalled 1,599,158 (up to the end of 1960).

**Although in a filthy condition, and then 15 months away from withdrawal, BR rebuilt Patriot No 45531 was still carrying the name SIR FREDERICK HARRISON when pictured between duties at Crewe station in early July 1964.** *Alan Fozard*

Lieutenant Sir Frederick Harrison was a British army officer who was a General Manager (1893-1908) and also earlier Chief Goods Manager of the London & North Western Railway (LNWR). Harrison was also deputy chairman of the South Eastern Railway (SER) for a period.

BR No 45531 is pictured on the turntable at Carlisle Upperby depot on 30/08/64. The loco is in a very unkempt condition but some well meaning person has rubbed away the grime from the bottom right hand corner of the cab to reveal a small section of the once splendid Brunswick Green lined livery. Note the cabside diagonal yellow stripe which denotes that the locomotive was prohibited from working south of Crewe under the then, recently energised 25kv overhead power lines, due to height restrictions. *Colour Rail*

Original LMS number **6011**, 1934 LMS number **5532**, British Railways number **45532**, the locomotive was named **ILLUSTRIOUS**. Loco No 6011 the Claughton locomotive it replaced (withdrawn February 1933) was also named *Illustrious* (from May 1923).

Built at Crewe, the locomotive entered service on 11 April 1933. This locomotive was rebuilt incorporation a Stanier '2A' tapered boiler, 17″ diameter cylinders, new smoke box, double chimney, new cab and larger Stanier tender re-entering service on 3 July 1948, new Royal Scot style curved and tapered smoke deflectors were later fitted. Principal shed allocations for this loco included Bushbury (09/1935) Crewe North (04/1944) Crewe North (02/1948) Camden (09/1950) Camden (10/1957) Carlisle Upperby (02/1964). The locomotive was withdrawn in February 1964, and cut up at Campbell's, Airdrie. Known mileage in service as a 5XP/6P loco 807,429 and thereafter 781,165 as a 7P loco, which totalled 1,588,594 (up to the end of 1960).

Illustrious is a long established name associated with British Royal Navy warships. A total of five ships have carried the famous name. The first of which was a 74 gun fighting vessel built in 1789 which having been damaged beyond repair during the battles against the French navy in 1793 was set on fire and abandoned. The next HMS Illustrious was another 74 gun ship which was launched in 1803 and after a long service career broken up at Portsmouth in 1869. The third ship of the line to carry the name was a 'Majestic Class' battleship with 12″ guns, launched in 1896 and scrapped in 1920 (LNWR Claughton 4-6-0 No 6011 was given the name in May 1923). The fourth HMS Illustrious was an 'Illustrious Class' aircraft carrier commissioned in 1940 and which served the Royal Navy until 1954. An 'Invincible Class' aircraft carrier launched in 1981 was the fifth HMS Illustrious (R06). A strategic review in 2010 has concluded that the vessel should be withdrawn in 2014. The ships motto is 'Vox Non Incerta' which translates as 'No Uncertain Voice'.

**BR rebuilt Patriot No 45532 ILLUSTRIOUS makes a fine sight heading a down parcels train at Shap, on the WCML in 1962.** *M Chapman/Colour Rail*

Original LMS number **5905**, 1934 LMS number **5533**, British Railways number **45533**, the locomotive was named **LORD RATHMORE**. Loco No 5905 the Claughton locomotive it replaced (withdrawn February 1933) was also named *Lord Rathmore*.

Built at Derby, the locomotive entered service on 10 April 1933. Principal shed allocations for this loco included Bushbury (09/1935) Camden (04/1944) Edge Hill (02/1948) Edge Hill (09/1950) Edge Hill (10/1957) Edge Hill (09/1962). The locomotive was withdrawn on 15 September 1962, and cut up at Crewe Works. Known mileage in service totalled 1,293,423 (January 1961).

Lord Rathmore (1838-1919) was David Robert Plunket, 1st Baron Rathmore QC who was an eminent Irish lawyer and Conservative politician; he was elevated to the peerage as 'Baron Rathmore of Shangahagh in the County of Dublin' in 1895. His association with the LNWR came about following that railway company's final acquisition of the North London Railway (NLR) in 1922, of which he was a director. In February 1909 the NLR directors gave over the running of their railway to the LNWR but the board stayed in post until the 1921 Railways Act precipitated a complete takeover of their lines and operating assets. Baron Rathmore was also a director of the Suez Canal Company and the Central London Railway (CLE) originators of the 'Twopenny Tube' (opened 1900).

LMS Patriot No 5533 LORD RATHMORE is pictured having just arrived at Euston station in March 1939. Plenty of railway activity in this image, the fireman is working on top of the tender whilst porters get busy emptying the parcel van. *J G Dewing/Edward Talbot Collection*

LMS No 5905 at Penrith with a down express service in the summer of 1933, the loco was renumbered in 1934. *Edward Talbot Collection*

LORD RATHMORE is pictured near to Rugby with a local service, in the summer of 1948. Note the words BRITISH RAILWAYS on the Fowler tender. Colour Rail

Original LMS number **5935**, 1934 LMS number **5534**, British Railways number **45534**, the locomotive was named **E. TOOTAL BROADHURST** in 1937. This name was also carried by Patriot loco No 5525 (45525) from 1933 until 1937. Loco No 5935 the Claughton locomotive it replaced (withdrawn February 1933) was unnamed. However LNWR Claughton 4-6-0 loco No 856 (LMS 5916) withdrawn November 1932) also carried the name *E. Tootal Broadhurst*.

Built at Derby, the locomotive entered service on 25 April 1933 (then unnamed). This locomotive was rebuilt incorporation a Stanier '2A' tapered boiler, 17" diameter cylinders, new smoke box, double chimney, new cab and larger Stanier tender re-entering service on 31 December 1948, new Royal Scot style curved and tapered smoke deflectors were later fitted. Principal shed allocations for this loco included Longsight (09/1935) Holbeck (04/1944) Holbeck (02/1948) Holyhead (09/1950) Edge Hill (10/1957) Crewe North (05/1964). The locomotive was withdrawn on 9 May 1964, and cut up at Crewe Works. Known mileage in service as a 5XP/6P loco 928,940 and thereafter 676,382 as a 7P loco, which totalled 1,605,322 (up to the end of 1960).

Sir Edward Tootal Broadhurst 1st Baronet DL, JP (1858-1922) he was created a Baronet in 1918 and is often referred to as a 'Cotton Magnate'. He was also the executive Chairman of the Manchester and Liverpool District Bank and a director of the London North Western Railway (LNWR) who also served as High Sheriff of Lancashire during the period 1906-1907.

**Rebuilt Patriot No 45534 E. TOOTAL BROADHURST is pictured on shed at Llandudno Junction in 1961. This loco was the second Patriot to carry that name as it was also carried by LMS No 5525 from 1933 to 1937.** *Mike Stokes Collection*

Original LMS number **5997**, 1934 LMS number **5535**, British Railways number **45535**, the locomotive was named **SIR HERBERT WALKER K.C.B.** in 1937. This name was also carried by Patriot loco No 5529 (45529) from 1933 until 1937. Loco No 5997 the Claughton locomotive it replaced (withdrawn February 1933) was unnamed. However LNWR Claughton 4-6-0 loco No 2204 (LMS 5926) withdrawn January 1933) also carried the name *Sir Herbert Walker K.C.B.*

Built at Derby, the locomotive entered service on 4 May 1933 (then unnamed). This locomotive was rebuilt incorporation a Stanier '2A' tapered boiler, 17″ diameter cylinders, new smoke box, double chimney, new cab and larger Stanier tender re-entered service on 25 September 1948, new Royal Scot style curved and tapered smoke deflectors were later fitted. Principal shed allocations for this loco included Longsight (09/1935) Holbeck (04/1944) Holbeck (02/1948) Crewe North (09/1950) Edge Hill (10/1957) Carlisle Kingmoor (10/1963). The locomotive was withdrawn on 26 October 1963, and cut up at Rigley's, Bulwell Forest. Known mileage in service as a 5XP/6P loco 963,187 and thereafter 663,552 as a 7P loco, which totalled 1,626,739 (up to the end of 1960).

**BR rebuilt Patriot No 45535 SIR HERBERT WALKER K.C.B. is pictured on shed at Willesden in August 1962. This loco was the second Patriot to carry that name as it was also carried by LMS No 5529 from 1933 to 1937.** *Gordon Stuart/Colour Rail*

**BR No 45535 is pictured at Ashton near Manchester on 19/04/62 with a heavy express service.** *C H Fairley/Colour Rail*

Sir Herbert Ashcombe Walker K.C.B. (1868-1949) was a railway company manager and company director of note. He was born in London and joined the London North Western Railway (LNWR) in 1893, initially fulfilling the post of District Superintendent North Wales Division. In 1902 Walker visited the USA to study American railway operating procedures on the behalf of the company. In January 1912 he became General Manager of the London and South Western Railway (L&SWR) and was instrumental in that railways introduction of electric traction. He received his knighthood in March 1915. From 1917 Walker served for a period as acting chairman of the Railway Executive Committee (REC) and was also made a Knight Commander of the Order of the Bath (KCB) in that year. He became General Manager of the Southern Railway (SR) in 1923 a position which allowed him to actively support further electrification of SR routes; he served the SR until the end of its existence in 1947. Walker, a strong supporter of the original channel tunnel plans, is commemorated by a striking cameo portrait set into a wall at London's Waterloo station.

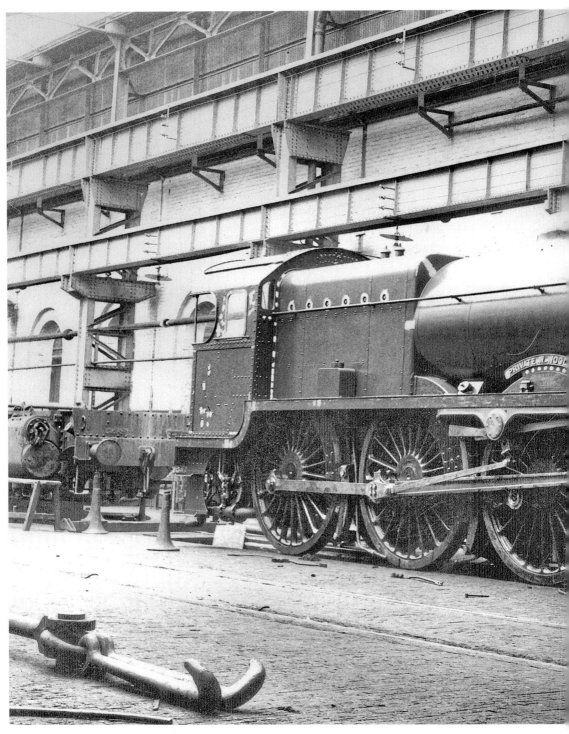

Under construction, LMS Patriot No 6018 PRIVATE W. WOOD V.C. (which became No 5536) is pictured in the erecting shop at Crewe Works during April 1933. *Edward Talbot Collection*

Original LMS number **6018**, 1934 LMS number **5536**, British Railways number **45536**, the locomotive was named **PRIVATE W. WOOD V.C.** in 1936. Loco No 6018 the Claughton locomotive it replaced (withdrawn February 1933) also carried that name, from April1926.

Built at Crewe, the locomotive entered service on 4 May 1933 (then unnamed). This locomotive was rebuilt incorporation a Stanier '2A' tapered boiler, 17″ diameter cylinders, new smoke box, double chimney, new cab and larger Stanier tender re-entering service on 12 November 1948, new Royal Scot style curved and tapered smoke deflectors were later fitted. Principal shed allocations for this loco included Longsight (09/1935) Preston (04/1944) Preston (02/1948) Longsight (09/1950) Longsight (10/1957) Sheffield Darnall (12/1962). The locomotive was withdrawn in December 1962, and cut up at Crewe Works. Known mileage in service as a 5XP/6P loco 843,884 and thereafter 700,976 as a 7P loco, which totalled 1,544,860 (up to the end of 1960).

Private W. Wood V.C. (1897-1982) was a soldier of the 10th Battalion Northumberland Fusiliers, who was born in Stockport, UK. The Victoria Cross (V.C.) is the highest most prestigious award for gallantry in the face of the enemy which can be awarded to British and Commonwealth forces. At the age of 21 and during the WWI battle for Vittorio Veneto (28 October 1918) in Italy Private Wood carried out the brave and selfless deeds which earned him his V.C. A British advance near to the town of Casa Vana was being held up by hostile enemy machine gun and sniper fire. Private Wood on his own initiative advanced with his Lewis gun and directed his fire towards the flank of an enemy machine gun nest (the military term for such an action being *enfilade)* his action caused 140 men to

**LMS No 5536 is pictured passing Rugby on 13/10/35.** *George Barlow/Transport Treasury*

BR rebuilt Patriot No 45536 PRIVATE W. WOOD V.C waits at Tiviot Dale station on 08/06/61. *D Forsyth/Colour Rail*

Stockport man and Newton Heath depot Driver Wilfred Wood V.C. is pictured with the loco that carried his name. Wilfred Wood joined the LNWR at Stockport in 1915 transferring to Newton Heath after war service he became a passed fireman in 1919 and a driver in June 1936.

surrender. Later during the same advance, after a hidden machine gun had opened fire on the Allied troops, Private Wood returned fire at point blank range and advanced singlehandedly towards the enemy position, he continually fired his Lewis gun from the hip as he did so. Having silenced the machine gun Private Wood, without waiting for further orders, took control of an enemy occupied ditch by raining fire upon it. This action subsequently caused a further 160 men and 3 officers to surrender. Wilfred Wood worked as a locomotive driver and the name plate from the withdrawn loco (No 45536) was placed on display inside Norbury Primary School, Hazel Grove until being transferred to the Northumberland Fusiliers regimental museum.

LMS Patriot No 5537 PRIVATE E. SYKES V.C. is pictured climbing out of Kendal with a Windermere-Manchester service. *A.E.R. Cope/Colour Rail*

Original LMS number **6015**, 1934 LMS number **5537**, British Railways number **45537**, the locomotive was named **PRIVATE E. SYKES V.C.** Loco No 6015 the Claughton locomotive it replaced (withdrawn February 1933) also carried that name, from April 1926.

Built at Crewe, the locomotive entered service on 19 July 1933. Principal shed allocations for this loco included Longsight (09/1935) Preston (04/1944) Preston (02/1948) Preston (09/1950) Carlisle Upperby (10/1957) Nuneaton (06/1962). The locomotive was withdrawn on 9 June 1962, and cut up at Crewe Works. Known mileage in service totalled 1,283,225 (end of 1960).

Private E. Sykes V.C. (1885-1945) was a soldier of the 27th Battalion Northumberland Fusiliers, who was born in Mossley, Lancashire, UK. The Victoria Cross (V.C.) is the highest most prestigious award for gallantry in the face of the enemy which can be awarded to British and Commonwealth forces. At the age of 32, and during the WWI battle for the control of Arras in France Private Sykes carried out the brave and selfless deeds which earned him his V.C. During that battle on the 19 April 1917 the battalion was pinned down by heavy enemy fire from the front and flank, the Northumberland Fusiliers were taking casualties at an alarming rate. Despite the heavy fire Private Sykes went forward and brought back four wounded colleagues. He then made a fifth foray into that extremely dangerous territory and remained there, in life threatening conditions whilst bandaging all those who were

BR Patriot No 45537 is pictured at Euxton Junction on the WCML with a Barrow–London Euston service in August 1949. Note that the locos Fowler tender was still lettered LMS at that time. *Edward Talbot Collection*

The end of the road, BR number 45537 is pictured in the old steel works building at Crewe works whilst being broken up in October 1962. *Edward Talbot Collection*

too severely wounded to be moved. During the Second World War Private Sykes, (a London & North Western Railway company employee) returned to serve with the 25th Battalion West Riding Home Guard. His V.C. is displayed at the Northumberland Fusiliers regimental museum in Alnwick, as is the locomotive's nameplate.

The proud family of Ernest Sykes are seen with one of the locomotives nameplates, which is displayed at the Northumberland Fusiliers regimental museum in Alnwick. Ernest Sykes was born in Mossley Greater Manchester and went to work for the LNWR as a platelayer until answering the call to arms in 1914. Following war service Ernest Sykes returned to the railways and served the LNWR and LMS for a period as a train guard. *David Anderson Collection*

Original LMS number **6000**, 1934 LMS number **5538**, British Railways number **45538**, the locomotive was named **GIGGLESWICK** in 1938. Loco No 6000 the Claughton locomotive it replaced (withdrawn February 1933) was unnamed.

Built at Crewe, the locomotive entered service on 21 July 1933 (then unnamed). Principal shed allocations for this loco included Longsight (09/1935) Leeds Holbeck (04/1944) Leeds Holbeck (02/1948) Edge Hill (09/1950) Preston (10/1957) Nuneaton (09/1962). The locomotive was withdrawn on 22 September 1962, and cut up at Crewe Works. Known mileage in service totalled 1,378,594 (end of 1961).

Giggleswick is the name of a Yorkshire village and prominent public school; the locomotive was named during a ceremony at the town's station. The locomotive name was bestowed in honour of the school, not the village. Founded in 1512, Giggleswick School received its Royal Charter in 1553. In this century it has expanded to become one of the leading independent boarding and day schools in the North of England retaining a national and international reputation. Giggleswick is a civil parish within the district of Craven, North Yorkshire. The parish church of St. Alkeda dates mostly from the 15th century but stones discovered during restoration work in 1890/2 indicate that a pre Norman Conquest building with religious significance probably existed on the site.

**LMS No 6000 seen when almost new, the loco is pictured resplendent in Crimson Lake lined livery at Kentish Town, whilst waiting to back down to head a Midland service off London St. Pancras station in 1934.** *P.S.Kendrick/Edward Talbot Collection*

BR No 45538 GIGGLESWICK is pictured on 24/06/61 between turns at Nuneaton shed. D *Forsyth/Colour Rail*

Original LMS number **5925**, 1934 LMS number **5539**, British Railways number **45539**, the locomotive was named **E.C.TRENCH**. Loco No 5925 the Claughton locomotive it replaced (withdrawn February 1933) also carried that name.

Built at Crewe, the locomotive entered service on 27 July 1933. Principal shed allocations for this loco included Aston (09/1935) Crewe North (04/1944) Crewe North (02/1948) Longsight (09/1950) Edge Hill (10/1957) Newton Heath (09/1961). The locomotive was withdrawn on 13 September 1961, and cut up at Crewe Works. Known mileage in service totalled 1,280,564 (end of 1961).

Ernest Frederic Crosbie Trench CBE, TD (1869–1960) was a British civil engineer who had a close association with railways. He was born to a noble family with his mother (Frances Charlotte Talbot Crosbie) being particularly well connected to British aristocracy. Trench studied at Trinity College Dublin for a Master of Arts degree. Thereafter he chose to pursue a career in engineering in general, and railway engineering in particular. He became an active associate member of the Institute of Civil Engineers in 1897, attaining full membership status in 1904. He was elected to the organisations ruling council in 1915 and served on it for the next 17 years, being elected vice president in 1924 and then serving as president between 1927/28. Trench was created a Commander of the British Empire (C.B.E.) for wartime services and further honoured with the Territorial Decoration (T.D.) after serving as a volunteer Colonel in the Engineer and Railway Staff Corps. In 1923 he was appointed to the post of Chief Engineer at the London, Midland and Scottish Railway, he retired from that post in April 1930.

**BR No 45539 E.C.TRENCH is pictured passing Stockport with a freight train on 08/06/61.** *D Forsyth/Colour Rail*

**BR No 45539 is seen in familiar territory, descending Beatock Bank on the WCML, at speed with a Glasgow-Carlisle stopping train on 09/07/60.** *David Anderson*

**LMS No 5539 E.C.TRENCH is pictured on shed at Aston in this 1934 image.** *Edward Talbot Collection*

Original LMS number **5901**, 1934 LMS number **5540**, British Railways number **45540**, the locomotive was named **SIR ROBERT TURNBULL**. Loco No 5901 the Claughton locomotive it replaced (withdrawn May 1933) also carried that name.

Built at Crewe, the locomotive entered service on 7 August 1933. This locomotive was rebuilt incorporation a Stanier '2A' tapered boiler, 17″ diameter cylinders, new smoke box, double chimney, new cab and larger Stanier tender re-entering service on 18 October 1947, new Royal Scot style curved and tapered smoke deflectors were later fitted. Principal shed allocations for this loco included Aston (09/1935) Crewe North (04/1944) Bushbury (02/1948) Longsight (09/1950) Longsight (10/1957) Carlisle Upperby (09/1961). The locomotive was withdrawn on 6 April 1963, and cut up at Crewe Works. Known mileage in service as a 5XP/6P loco, 642,953 and thereafter 813,599 as a 7P loco which totalled 1,456,552. (14/09/61)

Sir Robert Turnbull (1852-1925) was a major player during the growth of Britain's railway industry in general, and in particular during the development of the London & North Western Railway (LNWR) he was knighted in 1913. His father (also Robert) was the Vicar of Wybunbury, Cheshire at the time of his birth. Robert junior was educated at Whitchurch Grammar School in Shropshire and from all

**BR rebuilt Patriot No 45540 SIR ROBERT TURNBULL is pictured departing from Cheadle Heath on 08/06/61.** *D Forsyth/Colour Rail*

accounts he was an exemplary student. He joined the LNWR in 1868 and some seven years later became assistant district superintendent at Liverpool, moving to London to take up the post of Superintendent Southern Division in 1885. Two years later he became assistant superintendent of the line and then superintendent in 1895. He was promoted to the post of General Manager in 1914 but left that post in 1915 and joined the LNWR board of directors. He was also a director of the London, Brighton & South Coast Railway (LBSCR). In 1917 Turnbull returned to the LNWR so that his brother in law, Sir Guy Calthrop could be released from the company for war service as controller of mines (coal). Sir Robert was reportedly a very capable man, thus equally at home when tackling complicated railway financial matters as he was when presiding over development and research.

Rebuilt Patriot No 45540 SIR ROBERT TURNBULL is pictured in charge of 'The Comet', a titled express service which ran between London Euston and Manchester London Road (Piccadilly from 12/09/60). *Mike Stokes Collection.*

Original LMS number **5903**, 1934 LMS number **5541**, British Railways number **45541**, the locomotive was named **DUKE OF SUTHERLAND**. Loco No 5903 the Claughton locomotive it replaced (withdrawn April 1933) also carried that name.

**BR No 45541DUKE OF SUTHERLAND is pictured at Rugby Midland station on 24/08/60** *Keith Langston Collection*

Built at Crewe, the locomotive entered service on 15 August 1933. Principal shed allocations for this loco included Longsight (09/1935) Willesden (04/1944) Carlisle Upperby (02/1948) Camden (09/1950) Carlisle Upperby (10/1957) Nuneaton (06/1962). The locomotive was withdrawn on 9 June 1962, and cut up at Crewe Works. Known mileage in service totalled 1,311,227 (end of 1960).

The hereditary title Duke of Sutherland actually came into being in 1833. George, the eldest son of Lord Stafford by his second marriage (who had taken his father's title by succession) married Elizabeth Sutherland, 19th Countess of Sutherland. In 1803 he inherited the huge estates of his maternal uncle Francis Egerton, 3rd Duke of Bridgwater. In 1833 George Leveson-Gower, was created Duke of Sutherland in the Peerage of the United Kingdom. The first Duke and Duchess were controversial for the role they allegedly played in the Highland Clearances, when thousands of crofters were forced from their homes in order to allow sheep rearing on a large scale. George Sutherland-Leveson-Gower, the fifth incumbent, held the title when the Patriot locomotive was named in 1933.

## The LMS-Patriot Project

The aims of the LMS-Patriot Project as stated in its Memorandum and Articles of Association are:

- To advance the education of the public in relation to the 'Patriot' class of railway engines.
- To build, maintain, exhibit and operate locomotives of historic or scientific importance and in particular (but not limited to) a Fowler Patriot class steam locomotive.
- To encourage and facilitate knowledge of the history of the 'Patriot' class of railway engines, including the dedication of the class name in remembrance of the railway employee casualties of war with particular reference to the London, Midland and Scottish Railway and its constituent companies and British Railways and its constituent companies.
- To provide and facilitate historical and technical interpretative displays, materials and facilities, educational materials, study aids and educational events and opportunities of all kinds, using any form of media.

Visit http://www.lms-patriot.org.uk/

Locomotives 45542–45551 were built after 1933 and therefore did not have early LMS numbers, 1934 LMS number **5542**, British Railways number **45542**, the locomotive was unnamed. However this loco was allocated the name *Dunoon* which was never carried.

Built at Crewe, the locomotive entered service on 13 March 1934. Principal shed allocations for this loco included Longsight (09/1935) Patricroft (04/1944) Crewe North (02/1948) Carlisle Upperby (09/1950) Carlisle Upperby (10/1957) Nuneaton (06/1962). The locomotive was withdrawn on 9 June 1962, and cut up at Crewe Works. Known mileage in service totalled 1,254,703 (end of 1960).

**Double headed departure, unnamed BR No 45542 heads Jubilee Class 4-6-0 No 45700 AMETHYST in a spirited departure from Preston, with a down train on 14/04/61.** *Tony Gillet-Neil Dimmer/LMS-Patriot Project*

**LMS No 5542 is pictured with a down fast fitted freight at Watford Junction on 13/06/47.** *P Pescod/Transport Treasury*

1934 LMS number **5543** British Railways number **45543**, the locomotive was named **HOME GUARD** in July 1940.

Built at Crewe, the locomotive entered service on 16 March 1934 (then unnamed). Principal shed allocations for this loco included Longsight (09/1935) Patricroft (04/1944) Edge Hill (02/1948) Crewe North (09/1950) Carlisle Upperby (10/1957) Carnforth (06/1962). The locomotive was withdrawn 17 November 1962, and cut up at Crewe Works. Known mileage in service totalled 1,297,479 (end of 1960).

The Home Guard (initially 'Local Defence Volunteers' (LDV) or in slang, 'Look Duck Vanish', (hence the name change) was a defence organisation of the British Army during the Second World War. Operational from 1940 until 1944, the Home Guard, comprising approximately 1.5 million local volunteers (otherwise ineligible for military service) usually owing to age, hence the well known nickname 'Dad's Army', acted as a secondary defence force, in case of invasion by the forces of Nazi Germany and their allies. The force guarded the coastal areas of Britain and other important places such as airfields, factories, explosives stores and critical areas of the civilian infrastructure.

BR No 45543 HOME GUARD gets away from Derby Midland on 14/10/62 with the Derby-Northampton leg of the Midland Limited railtour, the little girl on the platform looks to be fascinated with the departure scene. *David Phillips/LMS-Patriot Project*

**BR No 45543 is pictured on the turntable at Derby prior to joining the aforementioned charter train.** *David Phillips/LMS-Patriot Project*

**BR No 45543 is pictured at Carnforth under a glorious blue sky in 1962.** *LMS-Patriot Project*

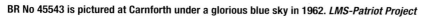

1934 LMS number **5544** British Railways number **45544**, the locomotive was unnamed.

Built at Crewe, the locomotive entered service on 22 March 1934. Principal shed allocations for this loco included Longsight (09/1935) Preston (04/1944) Preston (02/1948) Preston (09/1950) Edge Hill (10/1957) Warrington Dallam (12/1961). The locomotive was withdrawn on 9 December 1961, and thereafter cut up at Crewe Works. Known mileage in service totalled 1,259,905 (end of 1961).

**LMS No 5544 (which later became 5544 and then BR 45544) is pictured at Derby in this circa 1940 image.** *Mike Martin Collection*

1934 LMS number **5545** British Railways number **45545**, the locomotive was named **PLANET** in November 1948.

Built at Crewe, the locomotive entered service on 27 March 1934 (then unnamed). This locomotive was rebuilt incorporation a Stanier '2A' tapered boiler, 17″ diameter cylinders, new smoke box, double chimney, new cab and larger Stanier tender re-entering service on 5 November 1948, new Royal Scot style curved and tapered smoke deflectors were later fitted. Principal shed allocations for this loco included Longsight (09/1935) Camden (04/1944) Edge Hill (02/1948) Bushbury (09/1950) Crewe North (10/1957) Carlisle Upperby (05/1964). The locomotive was withdrawn 30 May 1964, and cut up at Connel's, Coatbridge. Known mileage in service as a 5XP/6P loco, 813,892 and thereafter 751,265 as a 7P loco which totalled 1,565,157. (03/05/61)

The name *Planet* was bestowed in honour of the 1830 Liverpool & Manchester Railway locomotive of the same name. The L&MR 2-2-0 *Planet* was built by Robert Stephenson & Company and is memorable in being the first successful inside cylinder loco. A working replica of that engine can often be viewed at the Museum of Science & Industry, Manchester.

**LMS No 5545 (at that time unnamed) is pictured as the 'train engine' double heading behind LMS Jubilee class 4-6-0 No 5623 PALESTINE on 03/04/34 with an up train at Gayton Loops (WCML).** *L Hanson/Edward Talbot Collection*

LMS No 5545 is pictured at Bletchley depot in May 1937, when in a really clean condition a proud locoman poses for the camera. *Edward Talbot Collection*

Rebuilt BR Patriot No 45545 PLANET is pictured outside Crewe Works in the company of 'Royal Scot' class 4-6-0 No 46110 GRENADIER GUARDSMAN, June 1957. *D. Forsyth/Colour Rail*

1934 LMS number **5546** British Railways number **45546**, the locomotive was named **FLEETWOOD** in 1938.

Built at Crewe, the locomotive entered service on 29 March 1934 (then unnamed). Principal shed allocations for this loco included Newton Heath (09/1935) Crewe North (04/1944) Crewe North (02/1948) Crewe North (09/1950) Crewe North (10/1957) Warrington Dallam (06/1962). The locomotive was withdrawn on June 1962, and cut up at Crewe Works. Known mileage in service totalled 1,212,897 (end of 1961).

Situated at the mouth of the River Wyre estuary, and some 7 miles from Blackpool, Fleetwood is one of Britain's chief fishing ports, holiday resort and sailing centre. Between 1841 and 1848, Fleetwood was a part of the 'West Coast

BR No 45546 FLEETWOOD pictured on shed at Crewe North on 19/08/61. The loco is in an exterior condition which was typical during the last years of steam. *D Forsyth/Colour Rail*

Main Line' (WCML) equivalent of its time. The fastest route from London to Glasgow was then by train to Fleetwood, and thence by packet boat to Ardrossan in Ayrshire. After 1848, the entire journey could be made by rail. The town's popularity owed much to the development of the railway, and from an early time ferry services were operated from the town's well appointed harbour to Belfast and also the Isle of Man. In modern times ferry services still operate to Larne in Northern Ireland. Fleetwood lost its rail connection in 1970, even though the local population led by their member of parliament fought hard to avert the closure. In 2005 the Poulton & Wyre Railway Society was formed in order to fight for the reinstatement of the town's railway link. Fleetwood is however connected by tram to nearby Blackpool.

BR No 45546 is pictured at speed along the WCML near Symington with a Liverpool/Manchester–Glasgow Central express on 14/06/58. *David Anderson*

1934 LMS number **5547** British Railways number **45547**, the locomotive was unnamed.

Built at Crewe, the locomotive entered service on 9 April 1934. Principal shed allocations for this loco included Newton Heath (09/1935) Edge Hill (04/1944) Edge Hill (02/1948) Preston (09/1950) Willesden (10/1957) Edge Hill (05/1964). The locomotive was withdrawn on 15 September 1962, and cut up at Crewe Works. Known mileage in service totalled 1,213,368 (01/05/61).

BR No 45547 is pictured as part of a three loco string at Carlisle. The BR 9F 2-10-0 is the loco under power, note that tenders of the Patriot and the Jubilee class 4-6-0 are empty tempting the question was this the end of the road for both of those locos? No 45547 was withdrawn from service in September 1962. *Colour Rail*

BR No 45547 is a credit to the cleaners, as seen at Llandudno Junction in 1958. Note the AWS battery box at the rear of the running board adjacent to the cab. *Keith Langston Collection*

1934 LMS number **5548** British Railways number **45548**, the locomotive was named **LYTHAM ST. ANNES** in 1937.

Built at Crewe, the locomotive entered service on 27 April 1934 (then unnamed). Principal shed allocations for this loco included Newton Heath (09/1935) Crewe North (04/1944) Crewe North (02/1948) Crewe North (09/1950) Crewe North (10/1957) Nuneaton (06/1962). The locomotive was withdrawn on 9 June 1962, and cut up at Crewe Works. Known mileage in service totalled 1,234,530 (end of 1961).

Lytham St. Annes was numerically the last of the resort named 'Patriots'. The naming ceremony took place at the town's station on 18 December 1937; this loco was one of 6 from the class to carry civic crests. Lytham, and St. Annes on the Sea, have over time grown together to form one popular seaside resort. Situated to the south of Blackpool the town stands on the Ribble estuary and boasts a restored windmill on its promenade. The town was served by the LMSR and is famously linked with international golf, amongst the nearby courses being Royal Lytham St. Annes. The area still has a rail connection as the 'Blackpool Branch Line' runs from Preston to Blackpool. The line diverges at Kirkham and Wesham junction, a double track branch runs to Blackpool North station (now Blackpool's main passenger station), while a single track branch runs to Blackpool South station and serves Lytham and St. Annes-on-Sea stations. Interestingly the town's name is often also spelt thus, Lytham St. Anne's.

BR No 45548 LYTHAM ST. ANNES one of six 'Patriot' class engines named after a seaside town is pictured in 1960 on shed at another seaside town, Blackpool Central. *Mike Stokes Collection*

1934 LMS number **5549**. British Railways number **45549**, the locomotive was unnamed. This loco was allocated the name **R.A.M.C** (Royal Army Medical Corps) but never carried it.

Built at Crewe, the locomotive entered service on 27 April 1934. Principal shed allocations for this loco included Polmadie (09/1935) Crewe North (04/1944) Crewe North (02/1948) Carlisle Upperby (09/1950) Carlisle Upperby (10/1957) Warrington Dallam (06/1962). The locomotive was withdrawn on 16 June 1962, and cut up at Crewe Works. Known mileage in service totalled 1,182,284 (25/10/61).

LMS No 5549 looks to be in fine fettle starting the climb from Oxenhope when departing with a down express circa 1940. *Edward Talbot Collection*

1934 LMS number **5550**. British Railways number **45550**, the locomotive was unnamed. This loco was allocated the name **SIR HENRY FOWLER** but never carried it.

Built at Crewe, the locomotive entered service on 1 May 1934. Principal shed allocations for this loco included Polmadie (09/1935) Patricroft (04/1944) Carlisle Upperby (02/1948) Carlisle Upperby (09/1950) Edge Hill (10/1957) Carnforth (12/1962). The locomotive was withdrawn on 1December 1962, and thereafter cut up at Crewe Works. Known mileage in service totalled 1,232,897 (02/11/61).

BR No 45550 is pictured on 01/02/61 shunting coaching stock at Birmingham New Street station. *D Forsyth/Colour Rail*

1934 LMS number **5551**. British Railways number **45551**, the locomotive was unnamed. This loco was allocated the name **ROTHESAY** but never carried it.

Built at Crewe, the locomotive entered service on 2 May 1934. Principal shed allocations for this loco included Camden (09/1935) Crewe North (04/1944) Crewe North (02/1948) Carlisle Upperby (09/1950) Carlisle Upperby (10/1957) Edge Hill (06/1962). The locomotive was withdrawn on 16 June 1962, and cut up at Crewe Works. Known mileage in service totalled 1,280,132 (end of 1960). This number will be carried by the new build Patriot locomotive THE UNKNOWN WARRIOR.

The aim of the Patriot Project is to build a new 'Patriot' steam locomotive to the original Sir Henry Fowler parallel boiler design; the new 3-cylinder 6P 4-6-0 will be capable of running on the mainline. The 'new' No 45551 named THE UNKNOWN WARRIOR will create a new 'National Memorial Engine'. The new build loco should be completed in time to commemorate the 100th Anniversary of the Armistice in 2018. The Royal British Legion are pleased to be associated with the project.

BR No 45551 is pictured on the WCML approaching Beattock Summit with an up Glasgow Central-Liverpool/ Manchester express, on 04/07/59. *David Anderson*

## Additional 'Patriot' class locomotive name information

During the war years (1939-45) the following names were allocated to 'Patriot' class locomotives, but thereafter not applied.

| LMS number | BR number | Allocated name | Additional information | Name actually carried |
|---|---|---|---|---|
| 5505 | 45505 | WEMYSS BAY | Clydeside seaside resort | THE ROYAL ORDNANCE CORPS (1947) |
| 5509 | 45509 | COMMANDO | Special Service troops | THE DERBYSHIRE YEOMANRY (1951) |
| 5513 | 45513 | SIR W. A. STANIER* | L.M.S. CME 1932-44 | No name carried |
| 5542 | 45542 | DUNOON | Clydeside seaside resort | No name carried |
| 5549 | 45549 | R.A.M.C. | Royal Army Medical Corps | No name carried |
| 5550 | 45550 | SIR HENRY FOWLER | L.M.S. CME 1925-31 | No name carried |
| 5551 | 45551 | ROTHESAY | Clydeside seaside resort | No name carried |

*Later applied to LMS Pacific No 46256, as Sir William A Stanier FRS.

During the period when the 'Patriot' class rebuilds were underway various other names were also suggested, but in the event never allocated to locomotives.

| Suggested name | Railway origin |
|---|---|
| VULCAN | Original LMS Royal Scot Class name. Carried by loco No 6133 from September 1927 to May 1936. Loco later named *The Green Howards*. |
| GOLIATH | Original LMS Royal Scot Class name. Carried by loco No 6136 from September 1927 to May 1936. Loco later named *The Border Regiment*. |
| COURIER | Original LMS Royal Scot Class name. Carried by loco No 6147 from October 1927. Loco later named *The Northamptonshire Regiment*. |
| VELOCIPEDE | Original LMS Royal Scot Class name. Carried by loco No 6148 from November 1927 to October 1935. Loco later named *The Manchester Regiment*. |
| CHAMPION | Originally an LNWR name carried by a superheated Precursor Class loco. |
| DRAGON | Originally an LNWR name carried by a superheated Precursor Class loco. |
| HARLEQUIN | Originally an LNWR name carried by an Experiment Class loco. |

Patriot No 45504 ROYAL SIGNALS hurries 'middle road' through Bromsgrove station with a Gloucester–Birmingham service. *Colour-Rail*

Patriot No 45539 E.C. TRENCH is pictured whilst double heading with LMS Ivatt 2-6-4T No 41271, the location is uncertain but the image may well have been taken in the Hellifield area. *Mike Stokes Collection*

A superb 1932 LMS scene, a down express is pictured passing Rugby. The train is double headed by North British built Midland Compound LMS No 1157 (became 41157 in 1948) and an unnamed, but unidentified, Patriot. *Edward Talbot Collection*

# Chapter 4

# STEAM LOCOMOTIVE BUILDING

In recent years various groups of railway enthusiasts have been formed with the stated aim of building 'new' steam locomotives, one such project is the plan to build an LMS 'Patriot' class 5XP 3 cylinder 4-6-0 locomotive. As in the case of the 'Patriot' class new build projects usually target the construction of popular locomotive designs of which no example was preserved.

Given the contemporary revival in steam locomotive building it is perhaps appropriate to briefly consider that very British tradition. Thousands of steam locomotives were built and operated in the UK over a span of 150 years. Divided into a great many classes and types the engines were produced by over 50 railway engineering companies and railway company workshops.

Basically iron ore was readily available and the technology to turn that into iron and steel well established. Simply put there were also good supplies of copper and brass, crucially the coal to fire the engines was also plentiful. Importantly the railways, and associated engineering undertakings, provided mass employment. The engineering skills which developed became the envy of the world, and it is true to say that Britain for a long period led the world in steam locomotive technology and construction.

It is hard to imagine how truly huge the railway industry which existed in Great Britain was, especially now that so little heavy engineering manufacturing capacity remains. To put things into perspective consider that at the time of the formation of British Railways (in 1948) in excess of 20,000 serviceable steam locomotives were collectively made available to the BR regional operating divisions. Well in excess of that number had been built, used in service and then scrapped during the preceding 100 plus years.

To fully appreciate the gravity of the tasks facing modern day locomotive builders and restorers it is important to understand that when the great railway workshops stopped building steam locomotives they also sent for scrap almost all of the custom built specialist machinery. Accordingly the majority of the workers together with their collective skills sadly became surplus to requirements. In what, with the benefit of hindsight, seems to have been almost indecent haste the railway works were disbanded, or reduced to shadows of their former selves in a relatively short space of time.

The main locomotive works associated with the LMS, and thus the 'Patriot' class of locomotives were based at Crewe and Derby.

| | Crewe Locomotive Works | Derby Locomotive Works |
| --- | --- | --- |
| Founded | 1843 for the Grand Junction Railway Became part of the London North Western Railway in 1846 and the London Midland & Scottish Railway in 1923, BR in 1948, British Rail Engineering Ltd in 1970 and later passed into private ownership. A small section of the works still operated as a repair facility in 2011 as a part of Bombardier Transportation. Steam engineers LNWR Heritage Ltd occupy a site adjacent to the former location of Crewe North depot. | 1840 for the North Midland Railway. Became part of the Midland Railway in 1844 and the London Midland & Scottish Railway in 1923, BR in 1948. The works became part of British Rail Engineering Ltd in 1970 and later passed into private ownership. The 'works' ceased to operate in 2004. However Derby Litchfield Lane carriage and wagon works was in use during 2011 as a part of Bombardier Transportation. |
| Steam locomotives | Total built 7,331 | Total built 2,995 |
| Last steam loco | BR 9F 2-10-0 No 92250, December 1958 | BR Class 5 4-6-0 No 73154, June 1957 |
| 'Patriots' built 11/1930–05/1934 | (40) 5502-19, 5523/24, 5529-32, 5536-51 | (12) 5500/1, 5520-22, 5525-28, 5533-5535 |
| 'Rebuilt Patriots' 10/1946–01/1949 | (18) 45512, 45514, 45521-23, 45525-45532, 45534-36, 45540, 45545 | |

The London and North Western Railway (LNWR) introduced the 'Claughton' class of 4-cylinder express passenger 4-6-0 steam locomotives in 1913 and a total of 130 examples were built at Crewe Works, up to 1921. The class was named in recognition of the fact that Sir Gilbert Claughton was LNWR Chairman at that time.

Initially the LNWR used a haphazard series of numbers which had previously been carried by withdrawn locomotives; however the London Midland & Scottish Railway (LMS) renumbered the class in the series 5900 to 6029. Twenty of the class were later rebuilt with enlarged boilers, whilst ten were fitted with Caprotti valve gear. The 'Patriot' class owes its origins to the 'Claughtons'.

Locomotive No 5966 is pictured 'on shed' at an unknown location in the mid 1920's, named BUNSEN. The name and number being allocated to LMS 'Claughton' 5XP rebuild No 5912 in August 1932 and subsequently BR 'Patriot' No 45512, which was rebuilt by BR to '7P' power classification in July 1948. *Dr Ian C Allen/Transport Treasury*

Crewe Works had its own self contained steel works and produced for the LMS all the required heavy drop stampings and forgings. It also produced most of the heavy steel components used in the manufacture of track and various other railway structures. In this 1930s image molten steel is seen being 'tapped' into a crucible. *Keith Langston Collection*

The way it was….Crewe loco Works in the 1930s. Using coal gas, actually made at the works own gas making plant, these workers are fixing tyres to cast locomotive wheels by first heating with gas and thus expanding the tyre (hoop) and then allowing it to cool onto the wheel. The main section of this image shows a 'fixed' tyre in place as the wheel set is lifted clear. *Keith Langston Collection*

Locomotive frames being cut from steel plate using an oxyacetylene cutting tool. Note the unguarded drive belts against the back wall, in the modern era the Health and Safety department would no doubt have closed down the shop! *Keith Langston Collection*

Note the gentleman in the 'bowler hat'. The foreman looks on as his team get to grips forging a huge work piece using Crewe Work's 2000 ton hydraulic press. *Keith Langston Collection*

A locomotive wheel centre is being drilled to size on this 'Vertical Wheel Lathe', which was one of several such machines. *Keith Langston Collection*

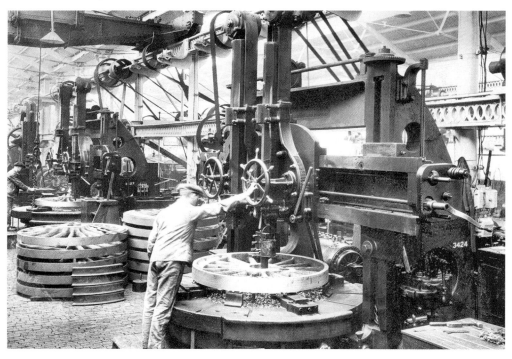

A huge 'Horizontal Wheel Lathe' once in use at Crewe Works. Note the work piece, it is a complete locomotive driving wheel set. *Keith Langston Collection*

In this 1930s image the wheel set is being balanced on a machine especially manufactured for that purpose. *Keith Langston Collection*

Steam locomotive assembly taking place on a grand scale, pictured in the Crewe Works erecting shop circa 1920. *Keith Langston Collection*

A finished boiler and firebox circa 1930, LMS new boiler construction was mainly centred on Crewe Works. *Keith Langston Collection*

This 1920s image of the Crewe Works machine shop shows that facilities intensive level of use to good effect; note again the large number of unguarded drive belts. *Keith Langston Collection*

This 1925 image of the steel works yard at Crewe Works helps to give an indication of the then overall size of the manufacturing facility. *Keith Langston Collection*

A refurbished BR boiler is pictured whilst undergoing an 'out of the frames' steam test at the works of London North Western Railway Heritage Ltd at Crewe in 2010. The Pete Waterman owned steam engineering company was commissioned to manufacture the boiler and firebox for the new build 'Patriot' class loco during 2013/14. *Keith Langston*

# Chapter 5

# THE PATRIOT PROJECT – NO 45551 THE UNKNOWN WARRIOR

LMS missing link! The creation of a new 'Patriot' class engine will effectively bridge an important preserved locomotive gap. Pictured at Carrog Station during the official launch of the project at the Llangollen Railway with preserved locomotives Stanier 'Black Five' No 44806 and Stanier 5MT Mogul No 42968 are front l to r Danny Hopkin railway writer and heritage journalist, David Bradshaw LMS-Patriot Project, back l to r John Buxton MD Cambrian Transport Ltd and supporter of the project, Andrew Laws LMS-Patriot Project Ltd and Richard Sant LMS-Patriot Ltd. *Steam Railway Magazine/LMS Patriot Project*

Since the 1960s steam locomotive preservationists have bemoaned the omission of several famous locomotive designs from amongst the otherwise comprehensive standard gauge mainline ex British Railways locomotives which were originally preserved, or subsequently rescued, following the end of the steam era in 1968. The total of ongoing new build British steam locomotive projects is expected to be into double figures as the 50th anniversary of the end of BR steam approaches.

Building a mainline steam locomotive from scratch with perhaps little else than unshakeable faith and a set of engineering drawings is a huge undertaking. Undoubtedly the A1 Steam Locomotive Trust set the bench mark for others to attain when following 19 years of hard work the 'new build' Peppercorn 'A1' class 4-6-2 locomotive No 60163 TORNADO steamed for the first time in 2008. A truly inspirational achievement!

The LMS 'Patriot' class engines in both original (and later rebuilt form) were extremely popular with the railway companies who operated them and the passengers who had rode behind them. Importantly railway enthusiasts also held the LMS 3-cylinder 4-6-0s in high esteem and greatly regretted the fact that none of the class of locomotives was preserved.

**Under the watchful eye of the ex Crewe Works Eagle!** Members of the Patriot group proudly show one of the nameplates for new build loco No 45551 THE UNKNOWN WARRIOR, on the occasion of the groups 2010 AGM held at Crewe Heritage Centre L to r Steve Blackburn – Engineering and Quality Director, Richard Sant – Project Director, David Bradshaw – Chairman Patriot Project and – Andrew Laws Sales and Marketing Director. *Keith Langston*

The 'A1' project proved that new examples of successful locomotive designs could be built, albeit only with massive monetary support. After a short period of initial campaigning the founders of the LMS-Patriot Project realised that a great many others shared their desire to bridge what has in preservation terms been dubbed the 'LMS Gap', by building a 'Patriot' 5XP 4-6-0 locomotive. Indeed by late 2007 it had become abundantly clear to the group that sufficient support existed for them to begin the serious business of building the new engine.

In addition to launching the all important public appeal the Patriot Projects principles got to work locating any suitable preserved locomotive parts. Finding original un-rebuilt 'Patriot' class artefacts would prove to be almost impossible, apart from locomotive nameplates etc which have lasting worth as collector's items, all of the 'Patriot' locomotives metal components were sent for scrap almost immediately after their withdrawal from BR service (approx 120 tons each of loco and tender). For example No 45500 PATRIOT was withdrawn in March 1961 and cut for scrap only a month later.

Fortunately there were other LMS locomotives preserved with component parts which were interchangeable with the 'Patriot' class engines. Sufficient to say that

The LMS-Patriot Project acquired a set of genuine ex LMS buffers. Two of the Buffers will be used on the loco which is being assembled at the Llangollen Railway Works and the other two are suitable for the ex Barry scrapyard Fowler tender which is currently being restored at Barry Rail Centre. The buffers were found on a rail-mounted crane which was being scrapped at the Great Central Railway (Nottingham) at Ruddington. *LMS-Patriot Project*

when loco No 45551 steams the collective practical help and goodwill of a large number of people within the UK steam locomotive preservation movement will be recognised as having been a very important factor in the ventures success. Accordingly public monetary support is crucial. Dreams can come true, but only at a significantly high cost!

The Patriot Project group had first to choose a number for their 'new build' locomotive. The aforementioned 'A1' group were able to use what would have been the next number in the British Railways Eastern Region series. That opportunity was not available to the new generation 'Patriot' class locomotive builders as the last of the class was No 45551 (LMS No 5551) and the first of the LMS Stanier 'Jubilee' class took the next number in the series, 45552 (LMS No 5552). Accordingly the decision was taken to use instead the number of the last 'Patriot' built No 5551 (BR 45551).

The group didn't want to create a replica of class leader, No 5500 PATRIOT (LMS 45500), because that engine was in engineering terms more of a Claughton rebuild (as was the second built 'Patriot' No 5501 LMS 45501) and as such both differed in a number of significant areas from the other 50 production Patriot engines. Following receipt of around 150 possible names for the new engine, after an appeal in the railway press, the five most popular choices were put to a public vote. The winner by some distance was 'THE UNKNOWN WARRIOR'. Accordingly the new build 4-6-0 locomotive has a totally new name and a reused number.

After a short period of initial campaigning the founders of the LMS-Patriot Project realised that a great many others shared their desire to bridge what has in preservation terms been called dubbed the 'LMS Gap', by building a 'Patriot' 5XP 4-6-0 locomotive. Original 'Patriot' design loco No 45503 is pictured. *Colour-Rail*

Members of the LNWR Heritage Ltd steam locomotive engineering team study the newly prepared 'Patriot' boiler and smokebox drawings. The new boiler will be of a traditionally riveted design incorporating a copper firebox. When complete, the new 'Patriot' boiler will be the largest built in the UK since 1960. Left to right Andy Tranter boiler maker, Richard Watkins boiler shop foreman, and Steve Latham works manager. *Keith Langston*

By negotiating with other locomotive societies, and trawling the archives of the National Railway Museum, a reasonable collection of engineering drawings were eventually located. To complete the 'set' additional new drawings were commissioned and were created by Pete Rich and the late Fred James. They will provide extra clarity, and fill in where originals simply do not exist.

The collection of ex BR scrap locomotives then in the ownership of the Vale of Glamorgan Council (and referred to as the 'Barry 10') were to prove helpful to the project as suppliers of suitable spare parts, in particular a Fowler 3500 gallon tender, of the type first used with the 'Patriot' 5XP locomotives, was made available. Although in scrap condition the tender was considered to be a suitable candidate for restoration. The tender from Barry Scrapyard was first dismantled and a new set of axleboxes ordered. The wheels were sent to Ian Riley Engineering in Bury for tyre turning and axle polishing and a new tender tank (widened from the original 7′1″ to 8′1″ to improve the water capacity) has been specified.

A decision was made to base the erection of the locomotive at the workshops of the Llangollen Railway, in north Wales. The basis of all steam locomotives are the all important frames and after drawings were specially prepared those items were

Restoration of the Fowler tender will be undertaken at the former EWS Depot at Barry Glamorgan, now the Barry Railway Centre. *The* Fowler tender is believed to have entered Woodhams scrapyard at Barry behind ex-LMS 2-6-0 'Crab' No 42765 in June 1967. When 42765 was bought for preservation, its tender, LMS number 3446, remained at Barry. *LMS-Patriot Project*

Agreement was reached with Cambrian Transport Ltd., the Project's biggest commercial sponsor, to overhaul the ex-Barry scrap yard Fowler tender that has been earmarked for use with 'THE UNKNOWN WARRIOR'. The tender frames will be restored to mainline condition by Cambrian Transport Ltd, using trainee apprentices and local skills in a joint scheme involving Barry College, The Vale of Glamorgan Council and Cambrian Transport Ltd. *Keith Langston*

ordered from Corus Steel and having been cut to shape in 2008 they were delivered to the Boro' Foundry in Lyle Worcestershire so that they could be drilled, in order to facilitate construction (as a pair). The birth of the 53rd 'Patriot' is thus judged to have taken place in March 2009 when the frames were delivered to the railway workshops at Llangollen.

The frames were ordered from Corus Steel Cradley Heath and were Plasma cut to shape in March 2009. *LMS-Patriot Project*

After cutting the frames were delivered to the Boro' Foundry in Lyle Worcestershire so that they could be drilled, in order to facilitate construction (as a pair). The frame plates were then transported to the nearby Boro Foundry where drilling and machining took place over 300 holes on each plate being drilled. *LMS-Patriot Project*

A set of 6 driving wheels became the next priority and the project group were assisted in this endeavour by Tyseley Locomotive Works who made available a pattern for the 6′ 9″ diameter castings. It was established that the wheels of the last ten 'Patriots' built were identical to those of the LMS 'Jubilee' class accordingly the pattern previously used during the restoration of No 45699 GALATEA was used to cast the driving wheels for No 45551.

Towards the end of 2010, following a successful public appeal for funds, the 6 wheels were cast by Boro' Foundry and thereafter delivered to South Devon Engineering, the company engaged to complete their manufacture. That work involved fitting one crank axle (which alone cost in the region of £20K) additionally manufacturing two plain axles, together with six crankpins, six tyres and the necessary balance weights. The total estimated cost of the driving wheel manufacturing process is approximately £80,000.

The project group have had help with regard to the required set of four 3′ 3½″ diameter bogie wheels. Donor locomotive Stanier 8F No 48518 ex 'Barry 10' provided one pair whilst the others have been recovered from a UK preserved Stanier 8F, which has in return received replacement bogie wheels from an ex Turkish Railways 8F. To complete the process new axleboxes and associated hornguides were cast for fitting into the frames.

A full set of motion was acquired many years ago from withdrawn Crewe built Jubilee No 45562 ALBERTA at the same time that sister engine No 45593 KOLHAPUR was acquired and some of this has been used to complete the motion

Towards the end of 2010, following a successful public appeal for funds, the 6 driving wheels were cast by Boro' Foundry. *LMS-Patriot Project*

After casting the wheels were delivered to South Devon Engineering, the company engaged to complete their manufacture. The final (6th) wheel is pictured after being machined. *LMS-Patriot Project*

The Llangollen Railway engineering team are pictured with the loco frames after fitting the drag box. The team will assemble locomotive No 45551 under the guidance of their Chief Mechanical Engineer Dave Owen (seen back right). *Keith Langston*

relating to the rescued 'Jubilee' No 45699 GALATEA by West Coast Railways Ltd, Carnforth, the surplus motion parts then being acquired for use on THE UNKNOWN WARRIOR. Advanced discussions were under way in 2011 with an engineering company in the West Midlands concerning the fabrication of the locomotives three cylinders. A new cab had been fabricated for display at the Crewe Heritage Centre and the associated smoke deflectors have now been manufactured and delivered to Llangollen.

The other major item is the boiler and firebox, which if donated funds permit will be built from scratch during 2013/2014 at LNWR Heritage Ltd works, at Crewe. The new boiler will be of a traditionally riveted design incorporating a copper firebox; a cost in the region of £80,000 is anticipated. When complete, the new 'Patriot' boiler will be the largest built in the UK since 1960.The frames will be completed by 2012, followed by wheeling, thus it is anticipated that the new Patriot will be well on the way to completion.

## National Memorial Engine

In January 2009, the group held successful talks with Stuart Gendall, the then Director of Corporate Communications, at the Royal British Legion. The LMS-Patriot Project obtained endorsement from the Royal British Legion (an internationally known charity which helps servicemen and women through their annual Poppy Appeal). The LMS-Patriot Project sought recognition in creating a

A joint dedication of the locomotive project which included an unveiling ceremony of THE UNKNOWN WARRIOR nameplate was held at the Llangollen Railway locomotive works on Monday November 2 2009. Following a dedication speech by RBL representatives, delivered in both English and Welsh a RBL bugler was called upon to sound 'the last post'. As the evocative strains of that classic lament echoed around the hushed locomotive works poppy leaves rained down onto the locomotive frames and union flag draped nameplate. Thereafter the union flag was smartly removed by a member of the honour guard in order to reveal the magnificent new nameplate. *Keith Langston*

new National Memorial engine, dedicated to the memory of fallen servicemen and women. The RBL's involvement will bring the project to a wider audience and hopefully will inspire a new generation of steam enthusiasts. In September 2010, the first print of a limited edition painting by Colin Wright was presented to the RBL and thereafter copies were offered for sale in support of the project.

The TORNADO Project captured the general public's imagination, by proving that new build steam locomotives can be successfully built in the UK. In building loco No 45551 the LMS-Patriot Project will fashion a new icon, a machine which will be more than just another steam locomotive. The new 'Patriot' class loco will be a fitting memorial and remembrance engine for the 21st century, in the same way that the original No 45500 'PATRIOT' was a memorial in the 20th Century to all the brave men and women who fought and died for their country in the Great War".

## Supporting the project

The LMS-Patriot Project raises money through regular monthly donations from supporters, and has also received some significant single donations from LMS enthusiasts. These donations have been supplemented by Gift Aid, where the Government currently contributes an extra 25% of the donation, from UK taxpayers. The Patriot Project are also seeking further 'Corporate Sponsors' and in addition are looking to raise income from legacies.

Donations can be sent to: 'The LMS-Patriot Company Ltd.', PO Box 3118, Hixon, Stafford, ST16 9JL.

A Membership and Regular Donations form can be downloaded from www.lms-patriot.org.uk or can be requested in writing, or by telephoning 01889 271058. Card donations can be made at www.lms-patriot.org.uk.

The Patriot Project is a Company limited by guarantee (Company registere.0d in England & Wales No. 6502248) that was formed to build a new LMS 'Patriot' class steam locomotive to the original Fowler parallel boiler design. The LMS-Patriot Project is Charitable Company (Registered Number 1123521). The LMS-Patriot Co. Ltd. Board consists of five Directors, who are also unpaid volunteers and Trustees of the Project. The new 'Patriot' is being assembled at the Llangollen Railway Works and will be certified for mainline running. All contributions from UK taxpayers can be increased by 25% if a Gift Aid form is included with the donation.

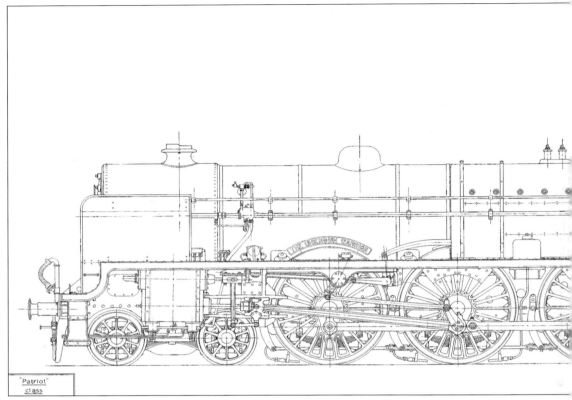

**A detailed engineering drawing of proposed new build locomotive No 5551 THE UNKNOWN WARRIOR, in LMS style livery.**
*Pete J Rich/LMS-Patriot Project*

| Numbers | Names | Numbers | Names |
|---|---|---|---|
| 5971/5500/45500 | CROXTETH, PATRIOT | 5958/5513/45513 | Unnamed |
| 5902/5501/45501 | SIR FRANK REE, ST DUNSTAN'S | 5983/5514/45514 | HOLYHEAD* |
| 5959/5502/45502 | ROYAL NAVAL DIVISION | 5992/5515/45515 | CAERNARVON |
| 5985/5503/45503 | THE LEICESTERSHIRE REGIMENT, THE ROYAL LEICESTERSHIRE REGIMENT | 5982/5516/45516 | THE BEDFORDSHIRE AND HERTFORDSHIRE REGIMENT |
| | | 5952/5517/45517 | Unnamed |
| 5987/5504/45504 | ROYAL SIGNALS | 6006/5518/45518 | BRADSHAW |
| 5949/5505/45505 | THE ROYAL ARMY ORDNANCE CORPS | 6008/5519/45519 | LADY GODIVA |
| | | 5954/5520/45520 | LLANDUDNO |
| 5974/5506/45506 | THE ROYAL PIONEER CORPS | 5933/5521/45521 | RHYL* |
| 5936/5507/45507 | ROYAL TANK CORPS | 5973/5522/45522 | PRESTATYN* |
| 6010/5508/45508 | Unnamed | 6026/5523/45523 | BANGOR* |
| 6005/5509/45509 | THE DERBYSHIRE YEOMANRY | 5907/5524/45524 | SIR FREDERICK HARRISON, BLACKPOOL |
| 6012/5510/45510 | Unnamed | | |
| 5942/5511/45511 | ISLE OF MAN | 5916/5525/45525 | E. TOOTAL BROADHURST, COLWYN BAY* |
| 5966/5512/45512 | BUNSEN* | | |

*Rebuilt

# 5XP locomotive numbers and names

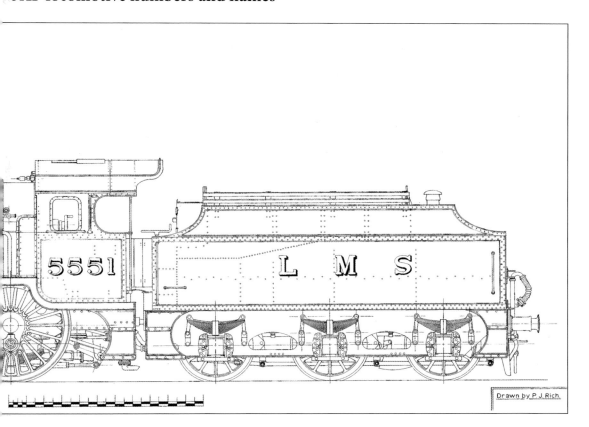

Drawn by P. J. Rich.

| Numbers | Names | Numbers | Names |
|---|---|---|---|
| 5963/5526/45526 | MORECAMBE AND HEYSHAM* | 5925/5539/45539 | E.C. TRENCH |
| 5944/5527/45527 | SOUTHPORT* | 5901/5540/45540 | SIR ROBERT TURNBULL* |
| 5996/5528/45528 | R.E.M.E.* | 5903/5541/45541 | DUKE OF SUTHERLAND |
| 5926/5529,45529 | SIR HERBERT WALKER K.C.B, STEPHENSON* | 5542/45542 | Unnamed |
| | | 5543/45543 | HOME GUARD |
| 6022/5530/45530 | SIR FRANK REE* | 5544/45544 | Unnamed |
| 6027/5531/45531 | SIR FREDERICK HARRISON* | 5545/45545 | PLANET* |
| 6011/5532/45532 | ILLUSTRIOUS* | 5546/45546 | FLEETWOOD |
| 5905/5533/45533 | LORD RATHMORE | 5547/45547 | Unnamed |
| 5935/5534/45534 | E. TOOTAL BROADHURST* | 5549/45548 | LYTHAM ST. ANNES |
| 5997/5535/45535 | SIR HERBERT WALKER K.C.B* | 5549/45549 | Unnamed |
| 6018/5536/45536 | PRIVATE W. WOOD V.C.* | 5550/45550 | Unnamed |
| 6015/5537/45537 | PRIVATE E. SYKES V.C. | 5551/45551 | Unnamed |
| 6000/5538/45538 | GIGGLESWICK | | |

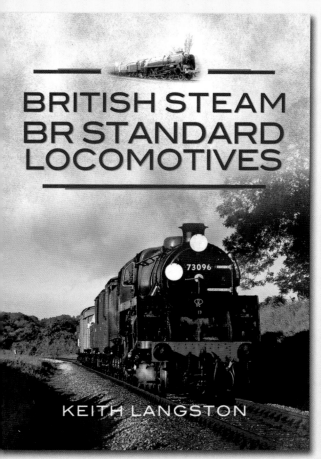